To Marclion, Miles & Logan:
Thanks for your love, support, encouragement &
understanding as I travel the world educating,
inspiring and empowering others to dream and
accomplish the extraordinary!

To Jonathan P. Hicks:
Thanks for your many years of advice, feedback,
support and the constant urging to, "Finish this
book...the world needs to read it!" Promise
made...promise kept! May you rest eternally in
heavenly peace!

4

ADVANCED PRAISE FOR THIS BOOK

"A spectacular book that uses an ingenious mix of insights and thought provoking metaphors as a means of providing clarity, focus and direction along the journey to both personal and professional achievement, while helping the reader avoid the land mines that seem to lurk at every corner of life. Jimmy craftily challenges the notion, why not, and why not me?"
- ***Harry Bonsu*** - *Senior Vice President, Administration, Independence Care System*

"*Dream Now* is an extraordinary example of how belief, grit and determination compliment the courage to dream, converting those dreams into realistic accomplishment for persons determined to trail blaze their desired path in life. *Dream Now* challenges our critical thinking process and inspires us to achieve what we set as our defining goals."
- ***Kim Hawkins*** - *VP & COO HEDCO, Inc.*

"*Dream Now* is an amazingly insightful guide for implementing personal strategies and achieving goals. It is required reading for anyone who seeks a better, more productive life and to help others reach their full potential."
- ***Reuben Shelton, Esq***. - *Lead Counsel - Litigation, Monsanto Company*

"As a linear person, I appreciate McMikle's approach to creating an easy-to-follow roadmap for becoming one's truest, best self. I found 'Dream Now!' to be a revelation and an important read for anyone looking for the inspiration and encouragement to step away from their fears and pursue the life they have longed to achieve. It's a great work."
- ***Michael J. Sorrell, Ed.D.*** - *President, Paul Quinn College*

"*Dream Now* is the right book for this season of life. It opens the door for great opportunities and possibilities conceived in the mind." McMikle has been a good steward over that which the Master has blessed him and he has laid out the vision for anyone to accomplish the extraordinary."
   - **Thomas L. Battles, Jr**. - *Grand Polemarch (National*
     President), Kappa Alpha Psi Fraternity, Inc.

"If you dare to dream and are willing to equip yourself with the tools to achieve your dream, you must read *Dream Now*. Each chapter offers all readers a road map to first recognize challenges, and then provides a clear and comprehensive series of best practices to achieve the desired goal. *Dream Now* offers invaluable insight and teaching moments for readers of all ages, backgrounds and occupations. Without question, this book will surely motivate all of us who dare to dream and seek support to make a positive life transformation."
   - **Joseph Bryant, Sr.** - *Public Safety Director, New Castle*
     County, Delaware

"A person's dream in life is central to the motivation it takes to become successful. Jimmy McMikle has touched a chord of life with an empowering simple strategy that we can all use. I sum it up with these words, "when our Faith Grows, Our Dream Grows and then WE Grow." *DREAM NOW! 10 Steps to Accomplish the Extraordinary*, is a must read for all persons, from the young aspiring trailblazer to the accomplished leaders of today."
   - **Dr. Marlon Mitchell** - *Executive Director, Institute for*
     Leadership & Performance Improvement

"*Dream Now! 10 Steps to Accomplish the Extraordinary* is a must read for your personal and professional growth. McMikle has the unique ability of tying together personal life lessons, quotes from historical legends and positive examples from successful doers and dreamers that masterfully instills, educates and motivates the reader to reach for his or her dreams, NOW!"
   - **Dr. C. Andrew McGadney** - *Vice President & Secretary of*
     the College, Colby College

"*DREAM NOW* is an inspiring, invigorating, motivating material that literally increases your adrenaline optimistically toward your goal and dreams in life. If you are ready for change and escalating movements, this book is for you. As you sail through the reading you will find your desires becoming more of a reality because *DREAM NOW* is designed to take you to your pinnacle of living. You deserve your dreams to come through so read to the last drop."

    - **Rev. Dr. Eric G. Garnes** - *Presiding Prelate, United*
    Covenant Churches of Christ

"This book offers a no nonsense approach to being the best you can be and provides a detailed roadmap to achieve your full potential while helping others reach their zenith."

    - **Samuel C. Hamilton** - *(Ret.) President & CEO, HEDCO, Inc.*

"Jimmy McMikle's life purpose is to play a meaningful role in empowering people to think BIG! In '*Dream Now - 10 Steps to Accomplish the Extraordinary*,' McMikle outlines an insightful template that will inspire youth and adults alike to chart their destiny."

    - **Stan Simpson** - *Host, The Stan Simpson Show-Fox 61 (CT)*

"*Dream Now!*" dives into a 10-Step process that makes you feel as though you're able to accomplish anything! The only thing you have to do is take the first step. *"Dream Now"* lets us know that we can live life to the fullest. Read this book and watch your cup 'runneth' over."

    - **June Archer** - *Entrepreneur, Motivational Teacher and*
    Author of "Yes! Everyday Can Be A Good Day", "Yes! You
    Can" & "After You Say, Yes!"

"This book will help people create their own path to success with a structured and focused game plan. Jimmy's passion to help others achieve greatness is shown on each page of this book."

    -Keshawn Dodds - *Director of Diversity & Community*
    Engagement, American International College

"This book, brilliantly done, is a must read for Charter School Leaders aspiring to overcome obstacles in the field of education! It causes one to be self reflective in their quest to achieve while emphasizing the value of hard work and the importance of having a vision that is louder than the naysayers. *Dream Now* is a blue print for developing a strategic plan that results in preparedness toward realizing your vision! *Dream Now* helps leaders recognize the power of collaboration and how to respond to *Dream Killers* when confronted by them."

 - **Dr. Troy A. Monroe** - *Executive Director, Jumoke Academy Charter Schools*

"This book is a great read. It combines a true reflection of the author's rise to personal success with practical examples of how others can achieve. College-aged students will learn and benefit from the examples provided. No one succeeds without the support of others."

 - **Larry Hall -** *Director of Admissions, Central Connecticut State University.*

8

TABLE OF CONTENTS

INTRODUCTION

I stood in my hotel floor hallway; patiently awaiting the elevator, which seemed determined not to arrive in any expedient manner. Pushed for time, I paced the floor hoping that the doors would soon open and I'd be on my way. As I waited, I glanced out of the hallway window, which provided a spectacular elevated view of downtown Phoenix, Arizona. Nestled amidst the varying heights and types of buildings on the downtown landscape, stood a particular structure that caught my eye. It was drastically different than any other edifice in the vicinity. The word dilapidated best describes my immediate thoughts. The top portion of the building was the only section visible from my vantage point, making it difficult to discern whether it was in a current stage of construction or in the process of being torn down. The structure was a gray cement block building without windows and strangely adorned with loudspeakers along the rooftop. The creative expressions of local graffiti artists were visually displayed along the front façade. Despite the many interesting facets of its physical appearance, the object that captured my attention was a phrase spray-painted on the building's right edge that read, "When we stop dreaming, we die!"

13

I wondered if the illustrator made a purposeful attempt at profoundness. Maybe he or she found recent inspiration in those words and felt the need to share that newfound wisdom in a vandalistic manner for the world to see. Perhaps the statement referenced the dying condition of the building itself, representing the failed realization of the dream for which the building was originally constructed. Whatever the reason, the statement captured (what I believe to be) a fundamental truth: "When we stop dreaming, we die!"

The cessation of dreaming doesn't produce an immediate death where one keels over and suddenly stops breathing, although that might be a better alternative. It produces something worse, a slow painstakingly miserable, deterioration of hope. Dream abandonment is acknowledgement and acceptance that life has soared to its greatest height and will never be better than its current state. When we stop dreaming, we relinquish the rights to the abundant life that we once dared to dream was possible to experience, settling for an ordinary existence in the face of extraordinary possibilities.

I believe that every person has the ability to, "accomplish the extraordinary;" to live a life of incredible measure and leave a lasting mark and legacy of greatness to represent their time spent on earth. However, that reality is only possible to the person who possesses a willingness to dream, the courage to pursue those dreams and the relentless determination to never stop dreaming.

Dream Now: 10 Steps to Accomplish the Extraordinary will help you harness the power of the dream that lies within you. It will inspire you to motivated action and empower your success. This book will reveal the ten steps that are critically important to unlock your unlimited potential and propel you towards your desired level of happiness and greatness, in proportion to your capacity to dream. Accomplishing the Extraordinary is a multi-stage process. You must:

1. Separate yourself from the "Dream Killers"
2. Insulate Yourself: Control Your Environment
3. Get Your Thinking Right
4. Dare to Dream
5. Dream Big
6. Dream Now
7. Persist
8. Empower Others
9. Inspire Others
10. Accomplish the Extraordinary

In the following chapters, we will explore each detailed step in a manner that will allow the practical application of each principle to your life and your quest. Get ready to experience their impact. You'll never be the same.

Dream Now is a book that contains words and chapters that are sure to change your life. The information contained in these pages may cause serious side effects. If you begin to experience excitement, enthusiasm, inspiration, motivation, drive, ambition or a sense of urgency to experience life in greater fashion; take a moment and gather yourself. You have probably been infected with the dreamer virus that this book is known to spread. It's highly contagious and difficult to cure.

You are about to embark upon an incredible life-changing journey. Are you ready? Let's get started. On your mark, get set, go and accomplish the extraordinary!

Chapter One – Dream Killers

*"Don't let someone who gave up on their own
dreams, talk you into giving up on yours."*
                                    - Unknown

I am reminded of the story of a 17-year-old graduating high school senior athlete, from a town in the Greater Hartford area of Connecticut, who excelled in the sport of track and field. The excitement of his fast approaching graduation was equally rivaled by the anxiety that surrounded the impending decision of where he would commit to a collegiate athletic career.

There were a number of scholarship offers and invitations, but no recruiting efforts were more frequent, persistent, and compelling than those from a local, in-state University (which shall remain nameless). The head coach (who we will call Coach X) painted a mental picture of a local boy who would become a statewide athletic hero. He would have the opportunity to etch his name in the record books, and be the catalyst for track and field growth at a place that needed his abilities and capabilities. It was a flattering, ego-boosting whirlwind courtship that led to a collegiate marriage proposal that ultimately required an answer.

Coach X received his reply one Wednesday night when he phoned the athlete's house. The coach, confident in the groundwork that he had laid to secure his potential top recruit's commitment, waited in eager anticipation to hear the collegiate choice made. To his surprise, the young man stated firmly, "I'm going to Indiana University." His answer created an extended, deafening silence, broken by one word, "why?" The athlete explained that he had a dream of competing for a major collegiate conference championship. He wanted the opportunity to compete for a team that possessed a good chance to win a national championship. He had Olympic dreams that could only be attained by the teaching, training, and tutelage of a major program that would provide exposure to elite competition. Indiana University was a nationally ranked track and field program at the time, with an incredible freshman recruiting class and a legendary head coach. Indiana invited him to be a part of that family. He knew it was the best fit for his dream.

Coach X uttered words in response that were both surprising and disappointing. They were words that one should never speak to another, especially an adult to a child. They were the proverbial smoking gun; the evidence needed in a court of law to convict a dream killer. Coach X explained that an athlete from a small town in Connecticut would (and could) never make a serious athletic contribution at a nationally ranked "Big Ten" university. Expecting success at Indiana University was a dream, a pipe dream. A Connecticut athlete would drown in that level of athletic competition. Coach X explained that it was important to understand that it is far better to be the "big fish in a little pond than a guppy in the ocean." Coach X instructed the young man to "swim in calmer waters." He advised the eager athlete to, "wise up and get a grip on reality." His cynical efforts continued until he finally realized that changing the young man's mind pertaining to his school selection was impossible. Coach X then hung up the phone abruptly.

The dream killer tried (regardless of his intent) to crush the hopes and dreams of a young man full of potential who believed that anything conceivable in the mind was possible if you're willing to work hard enough to achieve. He did so because he interpreted the athletes dream to be unrealistic. The athlete knew that a local college program could not provide a performance stage big enough for the athletic dream that lied within. Dream killers never understand the power of a

19

dream. Coach X tried to rob the history books of the story that was subsequently written. He couldn't envision the story of a Connecticut athlete who would become an important contributor to five consecutive Big-Ten (indoor and outdoor) track and field championship teams. But that story became true. He couldn't imagine that the record books at Indiana University would still bear the name of the athlete that Coach X labeled, "a guppy in the ocean," more than 20 years ago. But they do.

I tell that story because it is my own. It was the first time in my life that I remember facing a dream killer. It was the first of many dream killer encounters that I would experience in my life. Each occurrence would serve as a reinforcing reminder that not everyone who will occupy space in your life has your best interest at heart, or believes that you will be successful in what you're inspired to accomplish. Those encounters provided a sobering realization that people live lives with varying levels of belief, passion and zeal. People are motivated by different factors and belief systems but believe that their own concepts and principles apply to everyone else. If your dream doesn't align with their ideology, then they will try to deter you from your destiny. My first experience was the beginning of my understanding that a dream had to be bigger than those who would work to kill it. That example taught me a vital lesson in life. Don't let anyone steal your dream!

The power of a dream can overcome all of the naysayers, obstacles, challenges and pitfalls that barricade the road to success. Taking a leap and risking failure is always better than the subsequent conversation about what could have or should have been if only one had tried. Do not be paralyzed by the opinions of others. Do not be detoured from your destiny by those who lack vision, wisdom or courage. You are not the first person attacked by dream killers. Just like so many others, you are equipped to stand up against those attacks. Every significant accomplishment, discovery or creation throughout history has come to fruition despite an extensive list of dream killers who have prophesied and labored towards its demise. A dream killer's power is perceived, given life only by the dreamer who doubts; given validity only by the dreamer who succumbs to those doubts by failing to believe in him or herself. Always believe in your dream! Do not compromise its promise to satisfy disbelievers. You can accomplish all that you envision. Never settle for the crumbs of a dream when the entire cake is baking in your creative oven.

The Dream Killer Revealed

Every coach, sports enthusiast or competitive athlete is familiar with the mental imagery of a dimly lit room with a slew of coaching personnel gathered around a table, replaying athletic footage, evaluating statistics, and taking notes in attempts to obtain a competitive advantage. This scene is game planning in its truest form. Coaches and players alike spend hours a day each week watching and analyzing game film to understand the habits, schemes and tendencies of their opponents. There is obvious merit to strategic game planning. Effective scouting is a critical component of the game planning process. In fact, one can argue that there is no game plan unless observations from effective scouting have been accounted for and factored into game preparation. History has proven that the most successful teams and individuals consistently devote an inordinate amount of time to scouting their opponent. That practice offers an in-depth insight into the opponent psyche. By scouting, the opponent becomes predictable; thus, easier to understand, control, defend and defeat. Scouting decreases the opponent's significance as the obstacle and places greater emphasis on the execution of one's game plan to overcome the opponent's strategy and tactics. Preparation makes the game incidental. You've heard pregame interviews where the coach will say, "If we stick to our game plan and play according to our ability, we should walk away with a victory." There is a significant takeaway from that message. Take charge of your own success! Let your success ultimately depend on your preparation and actions, not that of others! As it is in sports, so true is it in life. Prepare yourself for the big game on your schedule with the dream killer.

I am fascinated by nature shows frequently aired on cable television that chronicle the life and culture of various inhabitants within the animal kingdom. I find it incredibly fascinating to watch animal scientists venture out into the wild to pursue and study some of the most dangerous animals and reptiles on the planet. It is easy to think that they have lost touch with reality by willingly operating in close proximity to these lethal beasts. But they see it differently. In their minds, they have a goal to accomplish. They recognize the associated risks and acknowledge the existing perils that accompany their quest, but understand that any worthwhile mission contains both. They clearly understand the danger but have learned to accomplish their goals despite ever-looming peril. Their poise under pressure is rooted in their preparation; the time spent studying the animals and the environment in which they will perform. It is their knowledge of the animal habits, tendencies and tactics that provide a level of protection and defense from the animals and other dangers (seen and unseen) that seek an opportunity to attack.

The animals in the wild represent the dream killers in your life. The dream killer is a perilous foe waiting to ambush you on life's winding road. Regardless of your level of awareness, you are constantly in the midst of dream killers! They pose an inherent danger to your life. If you learn to anticipate, avert, or elude the attacks that will inevitably come, you will succeed. Maintain poise in your life situations. Remain guarded, but unafraid and undeterred. You have tremendous goals to accomplish.

One of the most significant items on your success checklist is to gain familiarity with the dream killer's profile and purpose. You must understand the game plan, strategy and tactics that will be employed against you. The dream killer is an equal opportunity employer who will not discriminate against any dreamer because of race, color, religion, national origin, sex or age. The dream killer's mission is, "To reduce the ability, belief, confidence, desire, focus, and happiness of everyone, to limit potential and the realization of dreams! " Do not be naïve to the fact that the dream killer is a formidable opponent and that you are a target for attack. Fortify your defenses. Strengthen your weaknesses. Be impervious to dream killer strikes. Counter attack, launch your own offensive or avoid battles altogether. Learn to work smarter, not harder.

There will be many different names and faces associated with the dream killers in your life. Experience and exposure have taught me that they boil down to two types and five forms.

The Two Types of Dream Killers:

1. The Voluntary Dream Killer

Voluntary dream killers have destructive thinking and behavior patterns. Jealousy, envy, regret, negative perceptions or negative outlooks on life often motivate their mindset. Volunteer dream killers have grown comfortable with a consistent pattern of negativity. Negativity has become an ingrained response to any positive stimuli. They are eternal pessimists. A deeper exploration of the

24

dream killer psyche reveals a negative association of self. They hate themselves and find comfort with the practice of displacement, so you become a suitable substitute for their agony. You serve as a convenient dumping ground to empower their avoidance of self-introspection, self-confrontation and ultimately any change.

The voluntary dream killer will usually manifest him or herself in one of his or her more familiar personas, the "hater," the "bitter person," the "grump" and the "evil or miserable soul." Most voluntary dream killers are not difficult to recognize and identify. Interaction with this person often leads to a confrontational or offensive experience. They possess an outward adversarial or oppositional demeanor. They're easy to spot and a pleasure to avoid.

An additional and one of the most dangerous voluntary dream killers that you will encounter is, "the slickster." "The slickster," also known as "the backstabber," is not as apparent as the typical voluntary dream killer. This person may be someone with whom you have close ties or have developed an affinity. They gain your trust but build relationships based on deceit and ulterior motives. "The slickster" is a manipulatively wise individual who wants your dream for him or herself and seeks to obtain what you have and want.

2. The Involuntary Dream Killer

An involuntary dream killer is a well-intentioned person. He or she thinks that they know what's best for you. He or she honestly believes that they are offering advice, coaching or directing you in a manner that is actually beneficial to you and your situation. This person is convinced that the benefit of his or her wisdom will illuminate your dark path and redirect your misguided steps. They offer insight intended to provide a grounding influence, allowing you the opportunity to regain focus and accomplish their vision of success for your life. This person is not intentionally trying to kill your dreams. On the contrary, they believe in the concept of dreams. However, in the world of the involuntary dream killer, dreams fly at lower altitudes. The fear of failure destroys the courage of soaring to greater heights. This type of fear convinces the dreamer that a fall from a height above the clouds will hurt more than a fall from just below them. They opt for the "safe bet" or high percentage road to mediocrity.

The problem with the involuntary dream killer is simple. Their advice is based upon their off-based personal definition of reality, possibility, happiness and success. They are limited in their belief and narrow in their scope of comprehension of a person's abilities, capabilities and possibilities. The involuntary dream killer labels the truly successful as lucky and attributes notable success to luck or lucky breaks. There is no conquering spirit. Their story is familiar. They have either failed (following a lackluster attempt) or yet, have never found the courage or seized the opportunity to pursue their dreams. This dream killer is not bitter, but suffers from what I call, "Turtle Syndrome." Instead of taking risk and challenges, he or she retreats into his or her shell when facing the challenging opportunities and situations that life inherently presents, only to emerge in times of comfort and convenience. They want to swim and play quietly along the gentle waters of life's stream, avoiding the raging currents that ultimately make you a stronger swimmer.

The involuntary dream killer is also known as, "The Non-Believer," "The Defeated Soul," or "The Coward." This person is harder to recognize as a dream killer. They possess a non-confrontational nature. They appear friendly, sincere and often helpful, but will suck the life energy and ambition out of you that is essential to dream attainment.

Never evaluate your dream with their eyes. It's a losing proposition. Don't attempt to sell them the merits of your vision or seek their buy-in. It's a waste of time. They lack the mental capacity to comprehend the magnitude of any dreamer's imagination. Have faith in your dreams and lose the need for approval of the masses. Every attempt will end in bitter disappointment and delay. Remember that your dreams are your visions. The responsibility for delivery rests squarely on your shoulders. Don't let others redesign the building plans architecturally designed for your destiny.

The Many Forms of Dream Killers

My favorite television cartoon during my childhood years was, "The Super Friends." This animated series featured a group of superheroes that protected the world from the evil intent and actions of a collection of notorious villains who were determined to wreak havoc universally. Each superhero was endowed with a particular set of superpowers for use in their efforts. They ranged from the ability to fly to herculean strength, to amazing speed and to the capacity to exert mind control. Some superpowers were innately given, while others stemmed from the possession of a magic ring, belt or a similar symbolic article that empowered their characterization.

A set of biological fraternal twins called, "The Wonder Twins" existed in this superhero family. Although much younger in age, and less significant than the major superhero cast, they were still very effective when they sprang into action. However, their powers were slightly different than the typical superhero. They were individually powerless, dependent upon each other to unleash their powers. They would touch hands and utter the words, "Wonder Twin powers activate," to trigger the use of their superpowers. This deliberate, collaborative effort unleashed their ability to alter their physical shapes. The boy (Zan) had the ability to transform into any state and form of water (solid, liquid or gas). The girl (Jayna) possessed the capacity to transform into any animal form, assuming the strength and capabilities of that living thing. The two of them would appear as one thing, yet were quite different in reality. Their actual identity and agenda were revealed after they had neutralized or rendered their targeted adversary ineffective. In the case of the Superfriends, Zan and Jayna were agents for good. However, there are real life Zan and Jaynas in the world, who use their powers to kill dreams.

We have all encountered Zan and Jaynas in our lives; the people who disguised themselves in one form before the discovery of their true being became apparent. Oftentimes they were people that gained our trust and subsequently managed to foil our plans, alter our expectations or delay and detour our path to destiny. The dream killer plays the role of the wonder twins in our lives. He or she operates in close proximity to you, employing sophisticated measures of deception. You lose objectivity in your ability to analyze critically the significance of their negativity and ultimate catastrophic effect on your life.

Remember that (just like the wonder twins) the dream killer is powerless by him or herself. Your buy-in and belief are needed to activate their dream killing powers. Don't let them touch you. Don't give them power in your life! Recognize their various forms. The dream killers in your life will always disguise themselves in one of the following five forms:

1. Friends

The term "friend" is one of the most ambiguous words in the English language. Its meaning will vary per the individual who offers a definition. The Merriam-Webster dictionary defines a friend as, "a person who you like and enjoy being with: a person who helps or supports someone or something." However, many persons overlook the second portion of that definition, which is the most significant component of its meaning. For it is the second part that speaks to the positive, encouraging, uplifting nature that friendship should represent. Avoid befriending those persons who are fun, but void of constructive value to your lives. Dream killer "friends" are destructive because they are those with whom you choose to spend time. You like them. You welcome their opinions, suggestions, recommendations and feedback. That in essence is the problem. They plant seeds of destructiveness in your intellectual garden, which reap harvests of dream choking weeds. Supportive friends are assets, but befriending dream killers produce catastrophic results. Exercise extreme discernment in the selection of your friends. It is easy to evaluate a person by examining his or her closest group of friends. There is a proverb that says, "Tell me who your friends are and I will tell you who you are." This statement speaks to the fact that your closest cast of characters affects your performance and influences your outcome. Be careful with whom you select to spend time. Affiliate with purpose driven people and those sincerely supportive of you! The path to success will cause you to eliminate some friends and result in the loss of others along the way.

2. Family

The family unit is the fundamental building block of the communities in which we live. They provide a moral and ethical foundation as well as the early fulfillment of emotional, physical and economic needs. It is in the family unit where socialization begins, and where relationship development and spiritual and cultural heritage is introduced and reinforced. We obtain love, support and guidance from the family unit. They are the closest to you, the most familiar with you, and have the most direct and frequent access. As a result, they are the most comfortable expressing their opinions as it pertains to your dreams and your life's direction. A family dream killer associates the altitude of your dreams with their perception of your capabilities and promise. Their analysis may never be in agreement with your perspective. Don't be shocked to discover that the people closest to you can be the most destructive to your dreams.

3. Associates

This category includes co-workers and all other casual associates who occupy no level of real significance in your life, and have not ascended into the "friend" category. These are people that serve as a test. They test your resolve to remain focused. These people are not supposed to believe in your dream or care whether you attain it. They are the fair-weather people in your existence who expect you to fall in line with them. Don't expect any exuberance from them when you take the lead.

4. Authority Figures

This dream killer has a title position of authority over you. This person is most likely your boss (or someone in your supervisory chain), but can be anyone with sanctioned power from a legal or social structure. The fulfillment of your dream or elevation in any fashion threatens their position of power over you. Jealousy, fear of displacement or loss stimulates a suppressive effort to avert the loss of their control or the effectiveness of organizational structure.

Be wise and understand that ongoing efforts to support and assist you do not extend past the confines of the arena in which they have authority over your life. Do not expect the same level of support for the attainment of personal goals and dreams that they offer you in the course of your official association.

5. You!

At times, we succumb to the tricks and traps of others, but many times, the sole responsibility of idleness, underperformance as well as failure rests squarely on our shoulders. We have the potential to be the most destructive dream killer in our own lives. We sabotage our own efforts; not voluntarily, but when we fall victim to our *ears, fears and frustrations.*

Our Ears

We have all heard the saying by the Greek philosopher Epictetus that having two ears and one mouth means that we should listen twice as much as we talk. That idea speaks to the power of listening and the resulting learning process. That concept is true and great advice when you have been successful building a supportive circle of influence. However, no one is immune from persons who may infiltrate that circle and pollute the environment with cynicism. You have to develop discernment and a filter that mutes the verbal chatter of dream killers in your life. The dream killer is always willing to verbalize the difficulty, impossibility and lack of sensibility of your dream. They will highlight your deficiencies, imperfections and plant seeds of doubt and distraction in your mind that distort your purpose. Don't allow what you hear to take root and germinate.

Fears

My two children willingly share their dreams and their perceived picture of life when they reach adulthood. They speak to the massive nature of the house that they will occupy, the number and types of cars that they will own and the countless material possessions that they will obtain. My son wants to be a scientist, a professional football player and a zoologist. My daughter wants to be a dentist and a doctor. They sincerely believe it's possible to be all of those things at the same time.

The fascinating factor about children is their unswerving belief that anything is possible and that every dream is attainable. Their thought process is unpolluted and uncomplicated. It is simplistic, yet sophisticated in its level of clarity, confidence and conviction. Have you ever tried to reason with a child against his or her beliefs? It's a difficult undertaking. The negative opinions of others have no lasting effect on their determination. They are not intimidated by the challenge of the time or the obstacles to accomplishment.

As we age and mature, we trade in the belief of our dreams for a fraction of their possibility based on an adjusted perception of their likelihood. Our dreams take a back seat to the fears that we allow to drive as we gain comfort in the back seat progressing down the slow lane of life's existence. We settle with what we deem comfortable and familiar instead of what's imaginable. We succumb to fear.

Fear is a monster. It holds the belt. It is the undisputed heavyweight champion of self-inflicted dream killers. Every type and form of dream killer are effective by increasing levels of fear until that tactic prevents action. Fear is a natural emotion that even the most successful people experience. However, an unwavering dedication to purpose and a commitment to succeed despite those fears separates winners from losers. You must conquer three types of fears to be successful; they are fear of failure, fear of the competition and fear of the unknown.

Conquering the *fear of failure* is necessary. Your desire to want more has to outweigh the quality of life that you currently experience. Dismiss the notion that your inadequacies prohibit fulfillment of your dreams. It is important to understand that you will not be successful at every step or in every endeavor that you undertake. Every successful person can recount numerous stories of failure during their rise to their current position. But it was the lessons learned in those failures that developed their individual resolve and empowered their rise to the top.

You must conquer the *fear of the competition*. Inferiority, intimidation and doubt cannot flourish in the mind of a winner. Develop a warrior's mentality, a champion mindset and an inner confidence that you cannot be stopped despite the odds against you. Stop comparing yourself to others. Don't judge the probability of your success according to your perceived standing among those with whom you will compete. History provides countless examples of the underdog rising as the champion, the proverbial David versus Goliath. Your success has nothing to do with your competition. It reflects directly on your persistence to overcome the challenges that lie between you and your dream.

Never let *fear of the unknown* hold you hostage. You can never predict all of the tests and trials that you will face in your life. You will never know how you will respond to those challenges. But, you must grasp the reality that challenges will come and should prepare yourself to deal with them effectively. Chasing dreams will force you to step out of your comfort zone. It requires courage, sacrifice and faith. Never let fear of the unknown force you to hesitate and miss golden opportunities. Don't retreat or surrender to live a life filled with regrets.

My favorite poem is "Invictus," by the English poet, William Ernest Henley. He is a man who faced incredible adversity in his life. Saddled with family tragedy, health inflictions and professional challenges, Henley could have thrown in the towel. The development and acceptance of a defeatist attitude would have been understandable to most familiar with his life. Yet in his darkest hour, when his future was most uncertain, he penned the words of his most famous poem. This poem stands as an example of resilience and fortitude. The poem reads as follows:

Invictus:

Out of the night that covers me,
Black as the Pit from pole to pole,

I thank whatever gods may be
For my unconquerable soul

In the fell clutch of circumstance
I have not winced nor cried aloud.
Under the bludgeonings of chance
My head is bloody, but unbowed.

Beyond this place of wrath and tears
Looms but the Horror of the shade,
And yet the menace of the years
Finds, and shall find, me unafraid.

It matters not how strait the gate,
How charged with punishments the scroll,
I am the master of my fate:
I am the captain of my soul.

Despite the various challenges endured and the uncertainty of the future, a person's attitude, drive and perseverance always enable opportunity for success.

Frustrations

What happens when a dream doesn't happen fast enough or when the road to accomplishment is tougher than anticipated? Belief easily fades when goal attainment exceeds the desired time frame of expectation or amount of effort predicted. Belief also begins to wane when one does not receive a desired level of support. The result is frustration.

Frustration is an effective self-imposed dream killer that forces retreat and surrender. But, it should not. Accept the fact that your path to dream attainment will be longer, harder and more costly than you originally anticipated. Prepare yourself for that reality and govern yourself accordingly.

Identify the Dream Killers in Your Life

There may not be a dream killer in every category of your life, but when they appear, it will be in one of the previously described types or forms. Your role is to identify them, guard your dream and separate yourself from them.

Every Friday night at my house (when I'm home and not traveling) is "family movie night." We gather in the basement in front of our big screen TV or in our bed and watch whichever movie my two children choose. One particular Friday we were watching Disney's, "The Lion King." This movie was one that we had watched several times, but this viewing was the first time that I recognized a number of dream killers with starring roles.

"The Lion King" is the story of a young African lion prince named, "Simba," who is heir to the throne as king of the jungle. He lived a great life, full of promise and potential in the land that was known as "Pride Rock." He found comfort and convenience basking in the glory of his life of royalty, knowing that one day he would indeed be king. The mental imagery of that picture changed when his wicked uncle (Scar) conspired with a band of hyenas in a murderous plot against his father Mufasa. Scar subsequently convinced Simba that he was to blame for his father's death and that the shame and responsibilities of ruling at such a young age were too much to bear. Simba consequently fled into exile. Scar assumed the throne, ruling Simba's kingdom with the assistance of the hyenas. As Scar ruled (Simba's kingdom), Simba found comfort in a distant land, hanging out for years in the company of his new friends and associates, primarily a warthog (wild pig) named, "Pumba," and a meerkat (virtually a weasel) named, "Timon!" Hanging out and living "the good life" with his new friends made it easy for him to shirk his responsibilities and ignore his destiny to be king.

Several years later, an adult Simba had a revelation, a breakthrough experience. His father's friend, "Rafiki," discovered him one day and led him to a lake in the midst of a grass field where he had an encounter with the spirit of his father. His father reminded him that he had strayed from his destiny of greatness. He stated, "You are more than what you have become." He advised him to return to Pride Rock, realize his dream and fulfill his destiny

Simba was the son of a deceased king; therefore, a king in reality, but he was ignoring his promise. He had wasted years of his life running around in the forest with pigs and weasels, singing the song *"Hakuna Matada,"* which means, "Don't worry, be happy." But, he should have been worried. His rightful place was to rule on Pride

Rock. He had always envisioned life as a king. He knew it was his destiny. His people needed him, but he was hanging out in the lowlands with pigs and weasels. He was destined to lead, but he was hanging out in the lowlands with those who were happy keeping him off-task. His purpose was designed to carry out the responsibilities that the history and traditions of his people placed on his shoulders. He was destined for greatness, but he was hanging out in the lowlands with those who were ignorant of his greater purpose in life.

Simba would triumphantly return to Pride Rock years later to defeat Scar and the hyenas and rule as King. But there is a message to understand in this example that I share for your benefit. The story of Simba is a perfect illustration of the various types and forms of dream killers at work in a person's life and how easy it is to be lulled into mediocrity if we are not aware of dream killer traps. Simba's uncle Scar was a family member and also an authority figure in his life. This "slickster" voluntarily worked to destroy Simba's birthright and dream of becoming king to claim selfishly the throne for himself. He planted significant seeds of doubt and distraction that forced Simba to delay dream attainment for a considerable part of his life. The hyenas represent the casual associates in Simba's life. They held no level of importance to him, but they seized an opportunity to assist the onset of his ill fortune for their personal gain, by working in conjunction with Scar.

Simba served as his own dream killer by giving into his ears, fears and frustrations surrounding the death of his father, and feelings of inadequacy in handling the responsibilities that would satisfy the fulfillment of his destiny. He should have mustered the confidence and courage to stand firm in the midst of all the existing adversity.

While in exile, Simba found a couple of friends willing to provide enough fun and distraction to perpetuate his cycle of dream abandonment and negligence. Friends who add no constructive value to your life will keep you off task. It's easy to waste years of your life in the company of your chosen associations before you realize all that you have sacrificed to maintain them. In Simba's case, it was his kingdom. I'm not implying that you are royalty or that you have a chance to be a king or queen, but I urge you to evaluate your situation. Greatness at some level exists inside of you. You are supposed to accomplish great things. Don't let the dream killers get you off track. Who do you spend time with on a regular basis? Who are you allowing to deter you from your place of greatness? Assess the friends, family members, associates and authority figures in your life. Are they empowering your success or hindering your progress? Do not let the pigs and weasels of the world sidetrack you from reaching your place of destiny. They don't understand the calling or purpose on your life. Do not allow yourself to be your own worse enemy. Be deliberate and driven in your direction.

My words to you are the same as those told to Simba by Mufasa; "You are more than what you have become. Remember who you are!" You are not an ordinary person. There is tremendous promise in you and a dream that must be realized. Don't make excuses! Don't listen to the banter of others. Don't hide in exile! Don't lie in the lowlands! Rule on pride rock! Don't succumb to the detours of destiny that lie and wait to sabotage the accomplishment of your dream! Identify the dream killers in your life and separate yourself from their influence so that you can accomplish your dreams!

42

APPLICATION EXERCISES

---

1. Who are the voluntary dream killers in your life?

2. Who are the involuntary dream killers in your life?

3. Name the purpose driven people with whom you affiliate.

4. Name the people who actively support you.

5. What steps are you willing to take to improve the quality of persons in your life?

6. Make a list of your fears. Develop a plan to overcome them.

Chapter 2: Insulate Yourself: Control Your Environment

"Keep away from people who try to belittle your ambitions. Small people always do that, but the really great make you feel that you, too, can become great."

- Mark Twain

One of the most important steps in building a house is the insulation installation process. Every high school science class student learns that heat flows naturally from a warm place to a cold place. In the wintertime, heat moves directly from all heated home living spaces to any adjacent unheated spaces. That includes areas such as garages, basements and attics, or out to the house exterior. During the summertime, heat makes its way from the exterior of the home to the house interior. Insulation provides a protective barrier against the outside elements that threaten the integrity of the safe, healthy and comfortable living environment that one desires. Fortified walls, ceilings and floors provide 360-degree resistance to that outside environment. A well insulated home allows less warm air to escape in the winter season and less cool air to escape during the summer months. The insulation reduces the amount of energy needed for heating and cooling. The better your level of insulation, the higher your home's efficiency rating (ability to conserve energy) and the better your quality of life.

The parallel to your life is that you have a personal efficiency rating that is determined by how effectively you insulate yourself from the people and factors that drain you of precious energy needed for dream attainment. Your personal energy equation is a combination of purpose, focus, direction, efforts and belief. Insulating yourself means taking control of your personal environment, limiting access and exposure to the distractions that deter you from your purpose and create a cooling effect on the fire that fuels your dreams. Create the safe, healthy and comfortable living environment that allows maximum use of your energy and empowers your success. This involves doing the following two things:

1. Create Space

Firefighters commonly use a phrase called, "time, distance and shielding," to describe a cautious approach when responding to hazardous materials situations that threaten the health and safety of their crews. Explained simply, if you minimize the amount of time necessary to come physically in contact with a toxic substance or environment, maximize the amount of space between you and that danger and implement all appropriate and available barriers to limit exposure, then you create a high probability of a successful conclusion. Many things in your life equate to hazardous materials, which create a toxic environment to your being. If you don't exercise time, distance and shielding, you will succumb to the effects that these dangerously toxic substances produce.

In chapter one, we discussed the many types and various forms of dream killers. There is an unquestionable need to exercise time, distance and shielding from these individuals. Dream killers provide a winter environment that will continually produce bitterly cold forecasts in your future. Keep their influence on the outside. Creating space means that you will have to tell some people in your life that there is no longer a place for them. It doesn't mean that you have to dislike them or exhibit hostility. But, you must make the decision to take charge of your life and no longer allow just anyone to occupy valuable real estate on the landscape of your life. The process of separation

47

from people is not easy, but necessary for long-term wellbeing.

Creating space doesn't end with individuals. It involves an evaluation of **all** the nouns and verbs in your life. Create space from the exhaustive list of people, places and things that provide a toxic environment to your existence. Analyze the various elements of action in which you engage to assess their usefulness to, or deterrence from your purpose. That includes an assessment of your commitments and responsibilities. Determine if you are overly committed to things that conflict with your process of dream attainment. If you're not careful, then you can easily devote most of your time satisfying the needs and agendas of others, championing their causes and neglecting your own.

At the heart of creating space is time management. A day contains but so many hours. When you subtract sleep time, family time, work, essential responsibilities and commitments, the actual time available to leverage productively is less than what one probably realizes. Time wasted with people and activities that have no productive value to what you need to accomplish compromise the realistic ability to deliver the results necessary to your meet your goals.

2. Build a Powerful Circle of Influence

There is a common adage that states, "Birds of a feather flock together!" This metaphor denotes the reality that people of like minds, characteristics, values, interests and goals tend to associate in similar groups. The overlooked significance of this statement lies in its inference to the power of circles and how associations contribute to your success or failure. The people needed in your inner circle are the contrast of those from whom you create space. Achievement oriented people flock together, building powerful networks that feed, uplift, support and empower each other. They have little time or tolerance for purpose deterring distractions. Purpose-driven "flocks" are the eagles that soar to unlimited heights.

Ask yourself, who do you flock with? Which types of birds characterize your flock? Is your time spent clucking around in the company of chickens? Or is it spent running around, "like a chicken with your head cut off," wandering aimlessly and without purpose anticipating a lifeless fall? Do you flock at the park with pigeons; content feeding off the bread scraps that life throws your way? Do you flock with ostriches, the flightless birds stuck on the runway of life with no ability to take off and limited to the heights that they would reach? Ostriches are the same birds that are famous for the notion of burying their head in the sand to escape the challenges and adversities of life. Remember, you can't flock with everybody! Weak circles offer poor perspective, immature insight and dangerous direction. It's time to start flocking with eagles that soar above the trivialities of life. Make the conscious decision to tell all of the appropriate persons in your life, "I'm not flocking with you anymore!"

49

As a member of the "John Maxwell Team," one of my mentors is the international best-selling author and leadership expert John Maxwell. He writes in his book, "The 21 Irrefutable Laws of Leadership," about the importance of the "Law of the Inner Circle." In this specific chapter, he discusses an individual's potential in direct relationship to the quality of those closest to him or her. He instructs the reader to evaluate his or her inner circle to determine if those members add value, bring complimentary gifts to the table and provide a positive impact. He urges the recruitment of persons of competence, character and chemistry to the inner circle.

Think of your inner circle as "red carpet" caliber persons placed on the dignitary list for the party of your life. Your personal VIP section has a limited number of chairs. Determine who has a reserved seat. Better yet, think of your inner circle as your Presidential cabinet. Who would you appoint to be your most trusted, powerful set of advisers to help you achieve your platform goals? A powerful inner circle is made up of persons who fall into distinct categories; mentors, advocates, people of influence and partners.

MENTORS

Mentors have a vested interest in your success. They are the persons who recognize your potential and seek to develop it and you, without any personal or hidden agenda. The benefit of their wisdom offers invaluable insight that provides pitfall avoidance strategies that experience has taught them. Mentoring is a relationship-oriented commitment that spans a significant length of time. Almost every leader of any major accomplishment credits, at least, one (but often many) mentor(s) as a critical part of their success.

It is extremely important to understand proper mentoring. The term, "mentor," is thrown around too freely for my liking when referencing persons who don't really qualify to hold such title. Persons willing to offer advice on a regular basis should not be confused with those who make the commitment to provide invaluable instruction and guidance that will accelerate your growth and expedite your success. A relationship with a quality mentor is one of the most significant associations that a person will experience in his or her lifetime. I place a strong emphasis on the word "relationship" and the continuously developing nature of the mentor-mentee bond. A mentor is someone who takes you "under their wing," personally committing time and energy to ensure your personal growth and development. The following story illustrates true mentoring.

I had the opportunity to meet a Hartford, Connecticut-based corporate president and Chief Executive Officer (CEO), who had a well-established reputation as a significant change agent in the Greater Hartford business community. He was a proven transformational leader, well respected for his service and accomplishments. We were on the opposite ends of most spectrums in our lives.

I was at the beginning of my professional journey, a "bright-eyed and bushy tailed" young leader campaigning for the presidency of the Hartford Chapter of a civic organization to which we both belonged. He was an esteemed past president of the local chapter and a current national officer of that same organization. I sought his support for my candidacy and asked for a few moments of his time whenever convenient to discuss my platform and obtain any words of wisdom that he might be willing to share. He offered me a 30-minute time slot at 6:00 AM in his office the following Monday morning.

The first five minutes of our Monday morning meeting were an exchange of pleasantries. To be respectful of his time, I jumped into the purpose of my visit, sharing my thoughts and plans during the next five minutes. I took copious notes during the next 10 minutes as he shared invaluable insight and offered advice for the leadership path I was determined to make. The final 10 minutes were an interactive discussion, instigated by a barrage of questions to which he was gracious to provide answers. This session proved to be an important start to a mentoring relationship.

The Monday morning office meeting ended with (what I'll call) a hefty homework assignment. I was tasked with refining parts of my political platform, doing some general research and making contact with a list of persons with whom I was instructed to converse. The official report of my efforts was due the following Monday morning at a 6:00 AM breakfast meeting that he placed on my calendar. That second meeting ended with another list of items needing completion before a third 6:00 AM Monday morning breakfast meeting the following week.

I was beginning to notice a troubling trend; I might be eating Monday morning breakfast at 6:00 AM on a regular basis. Keep in mind that (at that stage of my life); I was not aware that restaurants opened for breakfast at such an early hour. I learned a critically important lesson as I staggered into the diner the next Monday morning; the most productive and successful people begin tackling the day early. Dining in his restaurant of choice was a host of very important business people in the Hartford business community. I discovered that they greeted each day with the energy and enthusiasm that it deserves!

Those initial meetings were the beginning of a five-year series of morning breakfast meetings each ending with a homework assignment designed to develop my capacity to lead. At the five-year anniversary of our meetings, my mentor gave me a gift. He changed our meeting times to 7:00 AM. Five years later, he gave me two gifts, an 8:00 AM breakfast time slot and the stoppage of regular homework assignments. However, tasks were assigned as necessary. We replaced some of the breakfast meetings with dinner, social outings, family gatherings, etc., as our relationship grew beyond mentoring.

Almost twenty years after that 30-minute Monday morning office appointment, we still meet regularly. We talk (at least) a couple of times per week, and text regularly. We have traveled the speaking circuit together, inspiring and empowering lives across the country. I consider him a father figure. I credit much of my success to that seasoned executive who saw promise within a young man and decided to develop that potential with no ulterior motive. And he still provides constructive criticism, direction and guidance. That is true mentoring.

ADVOCATES

Advocates are the people in your life who like you, support you, publically promote you, stand up for you and often leverage their resources and connections to assist your success. They have made a conscious decision and sometimes a financial commitment of support for you. The major difference between a mentor and an advocate is the depth level of personal relationship and the commitment towards your personal development. However, close personal relationships often develop with advocates over time as the consistency of good counsel, time spent, and reliability and joint service increases. Advocates have bought into the promise of your dream, goal, or cause and would like to see it come to fruition.

PEOPLE OF INFLUENCE

"People of influence" describes a broad range of persons who may not fall into a mentor or advocate category, but offer strategic counsel that empower informed and effective direction and decision-making. They possess a specialized skill set, knowledge base or perspective that have afforded them a level of success worthy of emulation. People of influence are persons who possess character, competence and integrity.

PARTNERS

Partners are those who you have joined forces with to complete or accomplish a specific goal or dream. Your partner may even be your spouse, significant other or close friend. They have earned your trust and respect through proven loyalty and dependability. They are equally invested in the success of any specific or all endeavors and equally committed to their respective undertaking. Hold them accountable for their specific responsibilities.

Building a powerful inner circle is not just about taking. A reciprocal relationship must develop. Do not take without giving. The mentors, advocates, people of influence and partners in your inner sanctum are encircled to support you. You have a responsibility to be a person of influence in their lives. Make a commitment to add value to all of the people who have invested in your life or play a role in your path to success. There is an excellent chance that these individuals will be extremely important to you for a significant period of your life. Make sure that you demonstrate that appreciation.

A powerful inner circle is without dream killers, yes-men (suck-ups), leeches, critics and cynics. These persons are counterproductive. You are familiar with the dream killer, but acquaint yourself with the others.

Yes-men are not critical thinkers, they're predictable commentators. They offer advice or responses that are consistent with what you want to hear. They buy into your every word operating in blind support of you. Yes-men fear offending you or committing any offense that will result in a fall from your good graces. They are comforting. They appear to provide incredible support but are instead nothing more than ego boosting suck ups devoid of productive value. Yes-men appeal to the weak minded, insecure leader threatened by the credible, constructive input of others that may point out more effective or logical alternatives. Yes-men appeal to those who need to be right and are less concerned with handling matters the right way. Yes-men are generally harmless to you in the larger context of life, but wasted space in your inner circle because they will never offer an objective opinion, advice or provide the tough love or hard truth responses that everyone occasionally needs.

Leeches are similar to yes-men, but with a few additional negative associations. Leeches and yes-men both want to remain in your good graces. However, leeches seek some form of benefit or personal gain through their affiliation with you, hence the name, "leech." They will suck the life, energy and financial resources from you. They take and use with no intent of providing anything of value in return. Their motives for affiliation are strategically designed to gain something for themselves. They are untrustworthy at best, destructive at worse.

Critics are those persons compelled to offer consistent opinions on you and your circumstances whether welcomed or not. Critics provide verbal and mental abuse to your operating world. Such abuse is not framed in a constructive context. It is instead often designed to tear down hopes and dreams. There is some value to critics in your life (when you are mentally strong enough to handle them). They can be the fuel that drives you. However, they can't be in your inner circle (circle of influence). The persons in your inner circle will provide plenty of constructive criticism needed to keep you properly aligned.

Merriam-Webster Dictionary defines a cynic as, "a person who has negative opinions about other people and about the things people do; *especially*: a person who believes that people are selfish and are only interested in helping themselves." *Cynics* cast a shadow of doubt and negativity over your life that will forever hide the sunshine in your future forecast. Protect yourself from their elements.

The concepts of creating space and building a powerful circle of influence are the two largest factors in establishing an insulated environment from which to begin your quest to accomplish the extraordinary. I experienced an encounter with a woman on a plane that served as partial inspiration for this chapter.

The Plane Lady

Frequent travel produces opportunities to have fascinating conversations with random people. I recall sitting next to a middle-aged woman on a flight from my home airport in Hartford, Connecticut to Minneapolis, Minnesota. This person serves as a constant reminder to me, a shining example of an individual who has failed to exercise the concept of insulation properly and the regretful effects. The simple question of "How are you today?" sparked a conversation that opened a floodgate of emotion, resulting in what amounted to an impromptu therapy session for this lady during this flight. I'll summarize.

"The Plane Lady" shared the story of her life, its shortcomings and her disappointments. She spoke of blown opportunities and carefully planned roadmaps that were never followed. She was remorseful of how (she described) life had passed her by. She was very educated, articulate and had held a few important job titles in life. She spoke of her (still burning) lifelong desire to open the doors of her own business and about all of the times various factors influenced her not to or prohibited her from the pursuit of that dream. Fortunately, she had laid out all of the parts of her puzzle of life in clear focus.

Unfortunately, she just never bothered to assemble the pieces. The heartbreaking reason was that she followed the advice of her friends and family at every critical junction point in her life. Her inner circle had always talked her out of pursuing her dreams and she always found a reason to justify the acceptance of the dream-killing directives of those from whom she took advice. There were no mentors, advocates, people of influence or partners around her. Her inner circle consisted of dream killers, critics and cynics. Perhaps more troubling was the fact that not one of them had received any level of collegiate education, attained any significant level of accomplishment in their lives, realized their dreams or served as anything but an anchor to hers. Now, with more than half of her life behind her, she had given up on the concept of dreaming and the possibility that life could be better than it was at its current moment.

She asked my opinion of all that she had shared, to which I paused for a moment realizing that there was probably not enough time left within the duration of the flight to articulate all that she needed to hear. I instructed her to do three simple things. The first was to create space. I urged her to separate from the people, thinking, habits and current actions that were reinforcing her defeatist mentality.

The second instruction that I offered was to build a powerful circle of influence. Get rid of the people who serve as dream killers in her life. They had tainted her dreams and continue to poison her possibilities. I encouraged her to associate and affiliate with people who are aligned more consistently with her desired direction in life.

Thirdly, I told her that life is not over, and she should never abandon her dreams. I shared stories of the persons who readily came to mind who realized (what many considered) "an impossible" dream in their later years of life. I spoke of how Ray Kroc began his quest towards the founding of the McDonald's franchise in his fifties, and how Colonel Sanders founded the Kentucky Fried Chicken franchise in his sixties. I encouraged her to revisit her lifelong dream of starting her business. I told her that life is not over until dirt is shoveled on your coffin; strive to accomplish your dreams until that day comes!

Despite (what I believe to be) one of my best pep talks ever, it was too late. The damage was done and irreversible (only because she believed it to be). She was offended that I would suggest separation from her friends and family. She verbally lashed out at me for criticizing the people for whom she cared and defended their advice given as protective action. Unfortunately, the reality for her was that a lifetime of poor insulation and exposure to the harsh elements of life had ruined her personal efficiency rating. The energy that proper insulation protects was stolen. Her purpose, focus, direction, effort and belief were gone.

I was overcome with her rush of negativity. In the middle of her tongue lashing, I put on my headphones and listened to music the rest of the flight. I felt that sharing an hour of my life was more than enough time for someone who had given up on their own. It was time to insulate myself!

APPLICATION EXERCISES

1. Name the 10 people who occupy the most time and space in your life. These are the people with whom you are closest, or have the most frequent contact/interaction. Answer the following questions about those persons:
   a. Who brings value to your life and why?
   b. Who has a draining effect on your life and why?
   c. Who has an established set of lofty dreams and goals?
   d. Who has none?
   e. Who can you count on in your time of need?

2. Identify the positive persons in your circle of influence. Answer the following questions about those persons:
   a. Who has committed to provide effective mentoring to you?
   b. Who are the advocates in your life?
   c. Who are the positive people of influence in your life?
   d. Who are the partners in your life?

3. Identify the negative persons in your circle of influence. Answer the following questions about those persons:
   a. Who are the yes-men (suck ups) in your life?
   b. Who are the leeches in your life?
   c. Who are the critics in your life?
   d. Who are the cynics in your life?

4. List your hobbies and/or chosen ways to spend free time.
   a. Which ones have a positive effect on your desired direction?
   b. Which have a negative or destructive effect?

5. Analyze your non-work or school responsibilities and commitments. Which non-work responsibilities and commitments:
   a. Have a productive effect towards goal accomplishment?
   b. Produce an opportunity for you to grow and develop?
   c. Are counter productive to your desired direction?

3

Chapter 3: Get Your Thinking Right!

"Whether you think you can, or you think you can't - you're right."

- Henry Ford

One of my favorite quotes is credited to Chinese philosopher Lao Tzu. It says, "Watch your thoughts; they become words. Watch your words; they become actions. Watch your actions; they become habit. Watch your habits; they become character. Watch your character; it becomes your destiny." This quote denotes an instructional watch item list to heed pertaining to the direction of your life. Pay close attention to the initial direction, "watch your thoughts!" Thought is the powerful catalyst that initiates and determines the ultimate direction of the cycle of occurrences that will happen in your life. The understanding of this quote links the magnitude of your destiny to the consequences of your thoughts and thought processes.

Positive thinking is the foundational base from which endless opportunities and possibilities grow. Consider "thought," the initial domino that must be properly positioned and aligned so that the remaining dominos of life fall according to design. The greatest plans, opportunities and promise are reduced to "would haves, should haves and could haves," by the absence of correct thinking. You will never accomplish your goals, reach your dreams or fulfill the potential of your promise until your thinking adjusts to the stage of believing that all things are possible and you are capable of making them happen.

The famous author James Allen states in his book, "As a Man Thinketh," that, "A person is limited only by the thoughts that he chooses." Positive thinking affords a level of control not accessible to the weak-minded or pessimistic individual. It affects your outlook on life, providing a "will to win," regardless of the circumstances and situations that separate you from your dreams. Positive thinking ignites an inextinguishable flame that yields a burning desire to surpass all imposed limitations.

Norman Vincent Peale instructs readers in his book, The Power of Positive Thinking, to "Formulate and stamp indelibly on your mind a mental picture of yourself as succeeding. Hold this picture tenaciously. Never permit it to fade. Your mind will seek to develop the picture... Do not build up obstacles in your imagination." In other words, define your vision of success and don't allow your thoughts to defeat you before your efforts have the chance to attain it. Ask yourself, what are you thinking? What obstacles have you erected or self-imposed limitations have you applied due to your thinking? Evaluate yourself to know.

Positive thought develops five traits that characterize dream-oriented thinking. Those five traits are: Belief, Confidence, Optimism, Passion, and Focus.

Belief

If "thought" is the foundation from which great destinies are constructed, consider "belief" the cornerstone that determines the position of the entire structure. Belief must be placed in proper position before any other facet of your life can line up accordingly. Doubt (and other forms of negative thinking) erodes the structure binding mortar of your being, causing continual deterioration towards an ultimate state of architectural ruin. Belief is the absence of doubt. Get your thinking right!

Belief begins with you! If you do not believe in yourself, no one else will. No one is forming a line to boost your ego. The world doesn't work in that fashion. You must see yourself as a uniquely gifted asset and a person of usefulness to the world. Determine your personal value proposition and have faith in its significance. Learn to rely on you. Never need anyone more than you need yourself!

Belief breeds high self-esteem, the manner in which you perceive yourself. There's a popular saying that states, "Perception is everything!" An individual's perception of self-shapes the geography of every border and determines the height of every ceiling in his or her future. Therefore, the perception of self will affect everything that one will ever do or become in his or her lifetime. Believing in oneself doesn't guarantee success, but the absence of it guarantees failure and a poor life experience. Lack of belief eliminates the ability to face life's challenges with any level of resiliency or confidence. Belief is a decision! Choose wisely!

Confidence

Belief builds confidence. Confidence is the belief in your own abilities and capabilities. It provides energy to pursue dreams, a readiness to embrace opportunities, the power to overcome challenges, poise under pressure and a willingness to endure. I challenge you to find at least one successful, dream attaining person who lacks confidence.

Optimism

The Merriam-Webster Dictionary defines optimism as, "a feeling or belief that good things will happen in the future: a feeling or belief that what you hope for will happen." My definition is, "the offspring of belief and confidence." The absence of doubt combined with an unwavering confidence in ability and capability affords one the positive outlook on life and sense of expectancy that dreamers possess. Belief allows one to think that something is possible. Confidence enables one to believe that he or she can make it happen. Optimism is the belief that it *will* happen, just as envisioned.

Passion

Passion is an intense desire. It's the fuel that allows your internal engine to run at high speeds for great distances to reach your desired destination despite the rough terrain, slippery roads and ever-changing weather conditions along the journey. Having passion is motivating; understanding what you are passionate about is therapeutic. Dreams are tied to passion. People without dreams don't understand their respective passions. Take 30 minutes tonight before you go to bed and make a list of the things for which you are passionate. I guarantee that list will become more defined by bedtime tomorrow night as your mind updates that list several times over the next 24 hours. I urge you to perform that exercise once again tomorrow evening.

Focus

Focus is the final and is arguably the most significant of the five traits of dream-oriented thinking. The first four attributes can be possessed and a person can still fail to accomplish his or her desired level of success. Belief, confidence, optimism and passion must be collectively focused on strategic action that is both efficient and effective. A person can spin their proverbial wheels, doing the wrong things in the wrong manner, wasting valuable time and energy to gain minimal results. Focus allows you to establish priorities, execute and fight situation-oriented distractions. Focus also keeps passion in order, allowing emotional restraint and sensibility. Aligning focus with the previously discussed four traits places your thinking in perfect balance.

Lao Tzu is also credited with stating, "Be careful what you water your dreams with. Water them with worry and fear and you will produce weeds that choke the life from your dream. Water them with optimism and solutions and you will cultivate success. Always be on the lookout for ways to turn a problem into an opportunity for success. Always be on the lookout for ways to nurture your dream." Now I'm telling you, "Get your thinking right!"

CHAPTER THREE
Get Your Thinking Right!

APPLICATION EXERCISES

---

1. What are your best individual qualities and assets?

2. Imagine that you will be introduced tomorrow to a live audience of thousands, with global television coverage. Write the introduction that will be used, which summarizes your **current** greatness in 250 words or less.

3. Revisit the scenario in question two, but the time is 10 years from now. Imagine that you have achieved the level of success and significance that you desire. Rewrite that introduction in 250 words or less.

4. Why should anyone believe in your ability to accomplish the extraordinary?

5. On a scale of 1 to 10 (10 being the highest), how much do you like yourself? _____
   a. Why is that your answer?
   b. What are you willing to do to improve your score (if not a 10)

6. On a scale of 1 to 10 (10 being the highest), rate your level of self-confidence? _____
   a. Why is that your answer?
   b. What are you willing to do to improve your score (if not a 10)

7. On a scale of 1 to 10 (10 being the highest), rate your level of optimism?_____
   a. Why is that your answer?
   b. What are you willing to do to improve your score (if not a 10)

8. Make a list of the things that you are most passionate about?

Chapter 4: Dare to Dream

"There are those that look at things the way they are, and ask why...I dream of things that never were, and ask why not?"

— **Robert F. Kennedy**

My wife and I traveled with our two children on a family vacation to Walt Disney World (and the other Disney Parks) in Orlando, Florida a couple of summers ago. I am of the opinion that most parents understand the fascination but are defenseless against the irresistible magnetism that the Disney brand has on all children. It's an addictive influence, an epidemic that has infected children globally. My kids are no exception. The Disney channel is a favorite on our household televisions. Disney movies line the bookshelves, while Disney characters, action figures and stuffed animals spill out of the toy boxes of our children's rooms. Their fascination started at an early age and it has yet to subside.

The announcement of our summer trip to Disneyworld left my children in a state of eager anticipation for months. In fact, they displayed a level of enthusiasm, focus and dedication towards this trip never exhibited to anything else during their young lifespans. They regularly consulted with each other, making trip plans, assembling their own "to do lists" of what needed to be seen and done during their time in the parks. My wife and I were given regular briefings of what was expected from us on this trip and we clearly understood the importance of "getting it right" for their enjoyment.

On that magical day of arrival, my daughter was especially overcome with excitement as we walked around the Magic Kingdom. Dressed in her Princess Jasmine costume, she could hardly contain her enthusiasm at the sight of the various Disney princesses that paraded throughout the park complex. Several hours later, she looked at me and expressed her desire that our family establish permanent residence at Disneyworld. She stated, "Daddy, I love it here...who would imagine making a place like this for kids?" My response was, "a man named Walt Disney." But I could have easily responded with the similarly correct answer of, "A person who dared to dream!"

74

If you have not had the opportunity to visit Disneyworld, I can attest that it's a magical place. In fact, a walk through any of the Disney parks is a virtual fantasy adventure. The creative genius is extraordinary. It's a place where imagination and creativity collide; leaving a playground that stimulates the senses and appeals to "the kid" in children and adults alike. However, the most important point to grasp regarding the wonder of Disneyworld is that it is simply the tangible manifestation of one man's dream. It's one of many examples that dreams can come true, for those who dare to dream. The Disney illustration is evidence that realized dreams have the power to influence and impact the world in a magnitude greater than previously imagined by the actual dreamer. The Walt Disney story demonstrates how dream attainment is a self-fulfilling endeavor and proof that a dream can leave a lasting legacy that blesses the lives and captures the hearts of future generations.

Dreams of that magnitude lie within you. Free your mind and unleash its power to dream. Daring to dream requires that you invoke two important internal elements: imagination and courage.

Imagination

The Merriam-Webster Dictionary defines imagination as, "the act or power of forming a mental image of something not present to the senses or never before wholly perceived in reality." Daring to dream accesses the far reaches of your creative mind, leveraging imagination.

Imagination is a powerful, motivating energy source. It's the proverbial key that unlocks the brain's ability to dream, initiating your march towards experiencing the life that you desire. Walt Disney stated, "First, think. Second, believe. Third, dream. And finally, dream." He understood the power of a dream, the belief in its merit and the continual need to leverage imagination to refine and inspire. He knew that imagination draws the blueprint from which a dream is constructed.

Disney also stated, "I resent the limitations of my own imagination," understanding that self-limiting thought, speech and behavior is self-destructive. External opposition, discouragement and negativity will emerge as you dare to dream. Don't create more. The only rule to dreaming is that there are no rules. Unleash the power of your imagination and ride its wave of energy.

Albert Einstein stated, "Imagination is more important than knowledge." He understood that the concept of knowledge is shaped by what is known, understandable and provable to the human mind. However, imagination allows travel beyond the definable borders of reality into unchartered territories of possibility. One can visit a place where the most far-fetched dreams have a chance of becoming true. Imagination gives you the ability and confidence to see past current positioning into the realm of conceivability. It offers the dreamer an opportunity to shape an ideal reality. Einstein said, "Imagination is everything. It is the preview of life's coming attractions." You have the ability to write the screenplay of your life and let the world marvel as it's played out on the big screen of history. Envision what your story will be. Determine the highlights. What special effects will be featured? What theatrical stunts will be performed? What is the dramatic climax? Let your imagination decide, and enable the chance for it to come true.

Courage

Far too often we are discouraged from dreaming. Dreaming doesn't fit into the practical nature of how society works. Dreaming places you outside of the box of predictability and conformity in which most people reside. Dreaming makes people uncomfortable. The dream killing "box-dwellers" resist the concept of dreaming and those who dare to dream, creating an environment of discomfort and unpleasant situations. But, never forget that you will have to gain comfort with being uncomfortable to dream. You will face difficulty, derision and uncertainty when you dare to dream. Step outside of the societal norm to experience life in the manner that your dreams decree. That will require courage.

Courage is the ability to stand firm in the face of any intimidating obstacle or challenge and muster the strength to defeat or overcome it. Courage is the "dare" in daring to dream. The first show of courage is feeling free to dream in the face of doubt, worry and our greatest self-inflicted dream killer, fear. Ambrose Redmoon stated, "Courage is not the absence of fear, but rather the judgment that something else is more important than fear." In other words, the hunger to eat has to be more motivating than the paralysis of being hungry or the fear of braving the dangers of the jungle to hunt. For what do you hunger? Make the decision that your dream is more important than anything that stands between you and its attainment.

The second show of courage is taking the necessary steps towards accomplishing your dreams. It includes an awareness of your personal obligation to achieve self-fulfillment and acknowledgement and acceptance of your commitment towards that goal. Understand that you (and only you) are responsible for the realization of your dreams. Sharpen your focus; become purpose-driven. Let your dream be the alarm clock that wakes you up every morning with a sense of determination and direction.

The third show of courage is remaining confident and resilient in the face of setbacks and detours that will occur along the road to dream attainment. Accept the experienced failures as valuable learning lessons that will strengthen your resolve. Realize that you will get knocked down, but you must get up, dust yourself off and continue your journey.

Imagination without the courage of pursuit is a waste of energy. Courage involves remaining steadfast in the pursuit of possibility in the ever-looming shadow of impossibility until your dream is realized. YOU have to make it happen!

Every now and then, I read something that leaves an impression on me. I came across the following poem, entitled, "Dare to Dream," by John Turnipseed, the Director of People Services at Southwest Airlines that speaks to the courage of dreaming. It reads as follows:

Some people only look at life,
through eyes that seldom gleam.
while others look beyond today,
as they're guided by a dream.
And the dreamers can't be sidetracked,
by dissenters who may laugh
for only they alone can know,
how special is their path!
But dreams aren't captured easily;
there's much work before you're through!
But the time and efforts are all worthwhile,
when the impossible comes true!
And dreams have strength in numbers,
for when a common goal is shared,
the once impossible comes true,
because of all who cared!
And once it's seen as reality,
a dream has just begun,
for magically from dreams come dreams,
And a walk becomes a run.
But with growth of course comes obstacles,
and with obstacles come fear,
but the dream that is worth dreaming
finds its way to the dear.
And the dream continues growing,

Reaching heights before unseen.
And it's all because of the courage,
of the dreamers and their dream.

Walt Disney stated, "All our dreams can come true, if we have the courage to pursue them." That mindset had to serve as a continual source of encouragement that allowed him to persevere in the face of criticism and ridicule. Imagine the boldness and bravery needed to combat the dream killer backlash during the 1950's, as he strived feverishly to transform a 100-acre orange grove in southern California into what is now celebrated globally as Disneyland. Who would have thought that the unbelievable magnitude of his vision, the perceived impossibility of his dream could occur, much less have such a global mesmerizing effect? However, Walt Disney was but only one person who dared to dream.

Who are the people that you consider the most successful? The only difference between you and them is that they have stretched the limits of their own imagination. They have dared to dream. Daring to dream isn't about qualifying the likelihood of the dream. It's about the courage to dream and the willingness to pursue that dream despite the probability of it coming true. Imagine what could happen in your life if you did both? I dare you!

CHAPTER FOUR
Dare to Dream!

APPLICATION EXERCISES

What do you dream about? Take the time to compile an exhaustive list of your dreams!

Chapter 5: Dream Big

"It always seems impossible until it's done."

– Nelson Mandela

A time-capsuled journey through the annals of history would reveal certain truths and consistencies. The most recognized and celebrated visionaries, difference makers, bold risk takers, heroes and geniuses that defied the odds to accomplish the extraordinary, were the same courageous dreamers who challenged the accepted view of what was feasible, to pursue a dream once considered impossible. They dared to dream, but chose to dream big, realizing that size does matter.

Big dreams produce big expectations, which motivate big steps towards generating big results. Big results have big impact and big impact changes the world. However, dreaming big carries a big price tag. The greatest achievers have faced the bitter criticism and disapproval of society. They have been labeled foolish, reckless and oftentimes insane.

One of the first history lessons taught in elementary school is that Christopher Columbus discovered America. His dream was to find new access to a distant land. Later lessons show us that his dream challenged many conflicting views of his time, including the "world is flat" theory. It was widely believed that his voyage would result in him sailing off of the edge of the world. Others thought that his men would starve to death before ever reaching his destination. His idea of reaching lands located to his geographical right by traveling left was deemed impossible. The societal consensus was that he was crazy. Embarking on such a suicidal mission was foolish. It was a big dream, but he never gave up until it was accomplished.

In the 1800's, Alexander Graham Bell had a dream that he could make sound travel over a wire, engaging persons in conversations that were geographically far apart. As an inventor, Graham had numerous failed attempts to deliver his product before finding success. His efforts were deemed a foolish waste of time. Everyone thought that he was crazy until he was successful, and they wanted their very own telephone.

The Wright brothers proposed and pursued the thought of human flight at a time when America was still fascinated by the novelty of the engine-powered car. These two brothers had the audacity to suggest the possibility of flight when society as a whole believed that birds were the only living creatures that belonged in the sky. They faced ridicule but remained steadfast in the face of adversity. They were thought to be foolish at best, but likely insane, until they took flight in 1903. Global airplane travel is now a regular, trusted component of life.

Big dreams are always crazy, at least until they come true. But when they come true, they deliver the amazing results that history documents as greatness. And the dreamers who dream them become the celebrated persons of their generation. It is your time to determine the dream for which history will celebrate you during your respective period of existence.

The three previous examples of big dreamers revealed two consistencies. To dream big, you have to do two things: Go crazy and Never Give Up!

Go Crazy!

Your dream has to be large enough to challenge current day thought of what's possible. Its size has to be big enough to spark occasional disbelief in your own mind, as the road to accomplishment proves trying. Its magnitude has to scare you at times! But always remember that big

85

dreams shape an extraordinary life. Small dreams ensure your place in the pool of mediocrity and commonality. Is your dream bigger than you? If your dream is safe, it's not big enough. If it seems easy to do, then it's safe and not big enough. If you know how you will face every challenge that will arise as you pursue that dream, then it's not big enough. If you think that you have it all figured out before you start, then it's not big enough. If people aren't shocked, amused or amazed at the audacity of your boldness, then it isn't big enough. The Spanish writer Miguel de Cervantes said it best, "In order to attain the impossible, one must attempt the absurd."

Go crazy with your dreaming! When people start to think that you are absolutely out of your mind with what you're proposing or pursuing, you have arrived in the land of big dreams. When your thought process is so unconventional that you lose friends and associates whose thinking cannot align with yours, your thinking has also arrived in the land of big dreams.

Conventional thinking yields conventional results, which are unacceptable to a big dreamer. Instead of settling for being average, settle on being imaginative, dedicated and committed to being an extraordinary person who produces extraordinary outcomes. The late author and poet, Maya Angelou stated, "A person is the product of their dreams. So make sure to dream great dreams. And then try to live your dream." Your legacy will be defined by your dream and the life commitment or effort that you make towards the accomplishment of that dream. How significant will that be? That's a question, which only you can answer!

At the heart of big dreaming lies the concept of possibility. Merriam-Webster Dictionary defines possibility as, "a chance that something might exist, happen, or be true: the state or fact of being possible." But, the definition of possibility is as individualized as the person who offers an interpretation. And, everyone's definition is correct because the probability of what's possible is tied to individual belief. The great dreamers are great because they see what others can't and pursue what others do not believe is possible. No one has the right to question or the ability to determine what's possible for anyone else, so don't fall victim to someone else's limits.

During the facilitation of workshops, I have been known to ask audiences to write down four questions. I preface those questions by establishing certain ground rules. I state that the boundaries of time, money, education, experience and any other resource of perceived need are not applicable to the exercise. I offer them time to answer the following questions:

1. If you could do or be anything in the world, then what would that be?
2. If you could have anything in the world that you truly coveted, then what would you want?
3. If you could affect change in the world as you desire, then what would you change?

4. What words do you hope are told about you at your funeral regarding the type of person you were, the life you lived and the things that you accomplished?

On the surface, these are four basic questions and seem simple to answer. But they are questions that many people never take (what I believe is the) appropriate time to answer. However, they lay important groundwork for the vision of your future. These questions tap into your personal realm of possibility. In order to dream without limits, one must remove the barriers or limitations at the onset of the dreaming process, to make his or her potential possible. Take the time to answer those four questions.

Never Give Up!

Every big dreamer who has accomplished the extraordinary has never given up on the belief that his or her dream is possible or in the effort to accomplish it! The big dreamer realizes that there is not an acceptable alternative. Settling for less than what is desired or expected is the equivalent of giving up. Giving up on your possibility sets you aimlessly adrift in the raging ocean waters of life, offering only regret and lack of fulfillment as the life jacket that will forever keep you afloat awaiting rescue.

The simple decision to never give up is an invigorating force that advances your cause, growth and development. The road to your dream includes a series of small victories and success stories that provide experience, encouragement, energy and strength along the way. The strength and wisdom gained from your struggles along that road prepare you to handle the success that accompanies dream fulfillment. Giving up robs you of that maturation process.

Never give up, because your big dreams are possible, but attainable only through a steadfast determination towards their realization. Never give up because compromising leaves you with a fraction of the life that you deserve and desire. Dream big, go crazy with your dreaming and never give up!

CHAPTER FIVE
Dream Big!

APPLICATION EXERCISES

1. If you could do or be anything in the world, then what would that be?
2. If you could have anything in the world that you truly coveted, then what would you want?
3. If you could affect change in the world as you desire, then what would you change?
4. What words do you hope are said about you at your funeral about the type of person you are & about the life you lived and the things that you have accomplished?

Chapter 6: Dream Now!

"We are now faced with the fact that tomorrow is today. We are confronted with the fierce urgency of now. In this unfolding conundrum of life and history, there "is" such a thing as being too late. This is no time for apathy or complacency. This is a time for vigorous and positive action."

-Dr. Martin Luther King, Jr.

I remember a discussion during a senior year English literature class at Indiana University about the poem by the great author Langston Hughes, "What happens to a dream deferred?" The poem in its entirety reads as such:

What happens to a dream deferred?
Does it dry up like a raisin in the sun?
Or fester like a sore --
And then run?
Does it stink like rotten meat?
Or crust and sugar over --
like a syrupy sweet?
Maybe it just sags
like a heavy load.
Or does it explode?"

- Langston Hughes

The classroom conversation intellectually dissected the profoundness of this poem and the theoretical analysis of its meaning and application. Some students offered explanations suggesting the symbolic reference to race struggles. There were others who presented notions that assigned meaning to any dreamer who fails to pursue his or her dreams while yet others saw it simply as the tragic discussion of the fate of unrealized dreams themselves. The brilliance of this poem is that it offers various philosophical questions that enable a timeless debate as to the specific intent of its meaning.

I remained uncommonly quiet during this particular discussion. The professor, surprised by my unusual silence looked at me and asked, "Mr. McMikle, we haven't heard your thoughts. What do you think happens to a dream deferred?" My response was, "What difference does it make, to the

94

dream that is...the tragedy is to the actual dreamer!" It was and remains my belief that in the case of unrealized or deferred dreams, the dreamer suffers the worst from the missed opportunity.

As people, we dream. We naturally explore the wants and desires of our hearts, imagining a wide variety of pleasing possibilities and successful outcomes. It is normal and gratifying to envision a life more substantial and satisfying than what we currently experience. The good news is that it's feasible to accomplish all that we envision. We have all been endowed with individual abilities and capabilities that enable us to advance towards and ultimately attain our dreams. Every dream that you can imagine, every desire, every good and perfect gift, every ambition of greatness is possible to those willing to do what is necessary for their attainment. The bad news is that life enters us into a race against the clock. We have but a small window of time on the earth to execute and accomplish something extraordinary. Some will, some won't. Your fate will be influenced directly by the decisions and choices you make and more significantly by their quality and timing.

Leadership expert Peter Drucker said, "There are two types of people, those who make things happen, and those who have reasons why they didn't make things happen." Which are you going to be?

Several factors separate those that, "actually" accomplish dreams and those that simply, "want to!" Among the most critical is a sense of urgency.

There is a proverbial saying, "Tomorrow is not promised," which highlights the vital importance of seizing opportunities, "Today!" Time is valuable and timing is critical. A sense of urgency inspires action, motivating the dreamer past the complacency and excuse making that defers dreams.

Apple executive, Steve Jobs is credited with stating, "Procrastinators who say, 'There's always tomorrow,' deny the reality that, one day, they will be wrong. Do something today that your future self will thank you for. It's easier to take a small action now instead of a big action 'some day.' What you do every day matters more than what you do every once in a while. If you really want to do something, you'll find a way. If you don't, you'll find an excuse."

Take charge of your life!

On a family vacation to the island city of Oak Bluffs, Martha's Vineyard, I walked into a downtown shop displaying motivational quotes, sayings, etc. I purchased a piece of art that now hangs in my bedroom. It was a quote by the late motivational speaker and author, Robert Moawed. The wording on that artwork reads, "The best day of your life is the one on which you decide your life is your own. No apologies or excuses. No one to lean on, rely on, or blame. The gift is yours, it is an amazing journey, and you alone are responsible for the quality of it."

This artwork is my daily reminder of who holds the ultimate responsibility for the direction and quality of my life...ME! And there is only one person ultimately accountable for your life...YOU!

That fact may be an unsettling thought for the person in denial, a sobering reality for the person waiting for handouts or help. But this fact should be encouraging to the person who has decided to take charge of his or her life. It should be inspiring to the person who believes in his or her own ability to accomplish the extraordinary. It should be empowering to the persons who will take matters into their own hands to ensure that they experience the extraordinary.

We exist as living beings to play the game of life with an extreme enthusiasm and passion to win, not to watch it pass us by. Stop spectating from the sidelines, huddled with the masses that have grown comfortable, "riding the bench," until the final whistle blows. Get off the bench, get warmed up, stretch out your muscles, get off the sidelines and into the game. One must first step on the playing field to satisfy any ambitions of being a champion.

There are defining moments and critical junction points in every person's life where choices or decisions made alter the course of direction for the rest of it. The decision to "Dream Now" changes your life for the better. Your next defining moment is NOW! Make the decision to take charge of your life. Take the following four steps:

1. Take responsibility

Be accountable for the matters that affect

97

you. The possession of a well-developed sense of personal responsibility is a mandatory prerequisite to gaining control of your life, and a necessary walking companion along your path to greatness. Take responsibility for where you are in life compared to where you want to be. Your current location reflects the quality of effort that you have made to this point in life. This stage represents the ownership step of taking charge of your life. It involves admitting to mistakes, learning from them and taking the steps necessary to not repeat them. You exit the excuse-making door and enter a room of self-awareness where self-improvement, individual growth and productive movement in your life become possible. Take ownership of your direction and the manner in which you will get there. Examine the situational circumstances of your positioning. Determine what is no longer acceptable and what is needed to advance. Give yourself permission to make the necessary changes.

2. Develop a plan

Many of the people with whom you affiliate don't have a plan on how to unlock their potential to accomplish the extraordinary or a clue to realize that they need one. But you must have both. Developing a roadmap that provides clear direction for the accomplishment of your dreams keeps you on target and focused on the tasks at hand on a daily basis. The poet Robert Burns says, "The best-laid plans of mouse and men often go awry." This statement highlights the realism that you will encounter potholes and detours on your road to accomplishing the extraordinary despite how well your plan is formulated. But, that's to be expected. Possessing a roadmap keeps you grounded, on track and firmly focused on the specifics of what you need to do. A plan allows you to get up after you have fallen and keep walking towards your plotted destination.

Have a clue! Stay clued into the warning signs and factors that will trigger the need to adjust and adapt to changing conditions and circumstances to remain on your charted course. Establish a set of goals that are specific, measurable, attainable, realistic and timely (S.M.A.R.T.). Develop a set of objectives or progressive action steps that allow you to accomplish your set goals. Prioritize activities and set benchmarks towards accomplishing each step.

3. Develop Self Discipline

Develop the self-discipline to follow through and complete the tasks that you begin. Self-discipline provides clear "big-picture" focus; a demonstrated level of self-control that provides a steadfast commitment to delivering, despite all of the challenges, deterrents or lack of desire. Self-discipline denies the instantaneous gratification that accompanies doing what you want to do, in deference to doing what you need to do to experience what you truly desire at a later date. It's an inner strength that is necessary to maintain structured direction. Do what you need to do!

4. Take Care of Your Self (3 things)

No plan stands a reasonable chance of being accomplished, no matter how elaborately designed, no matter how realistic in its approach, unless the person who executes is healthy enough to perform. It is not possible to take care of anything or anyone else effectively until you first take care of self.

Exercise Regularly

I would venture to guess that the average person is well aware of what he or she is supposed to do or what needs to be done as it relates to their personal health maintenance. Exercise is an important factor in that equation. I believe that if you stop and talk to any random person walking down any street, that they can list at least five benefits of a regular exercise regimen regardless of their personal level of exercise activity. The benefits of exercise are learned at an early age. However, too many persons fail to exercise the self-discipline needed to be consistent to obtain the benefits. Physical inactivity is a major contributor to the troubling obesity statistics that have become so problematic. Exercise is the preventative enemy of obesity. The health benefits are plentiful. I'm not a doctor, but life has taught me that regular exercise decreases the probability of cardiovascular disease.

It lowers levels of bad cholesterol, the risk of heart disease, high-blood pressure, stroke, diabetes and arthritis. It boosts energy and has positive effects on individual mood. Don't take for granted the opportunity to exercise.

I've been an avid runner for most of my life and known to play a little basketball, golf and tennis with "the guys" to keep fit. However, life threw me a curveball a few years ago in the form of a severe ankle injury that (following three surgeries) has ended my ability to exercise as usually accustomed. After a year on crutches, I had to rethink and relearn the concept of exercise. I had to find alternative (non-joint pounding) methods of exercise that now include walking and biking. During my long period of post-surgery rest and rehabilitation, I often read stories of persons who lost limbs and those who survived severe physical injuries who rebounded, refusing to allow their life to be shaped negatively by their experience, and now maintain a high level of physical fitness. I drew strength from their courage as I learned to walk again. Since that time, I've been able to maintain a regular exercise schedule despite the pain that I still experience every time I workout. I've been able to preserve a good level of physical fitness. In fact, one would never guess that I had an injury of such magnitude without my confession. I don't exercise because of a burning desire to sweat, pant and ache. I do so because it's an important component of my health and longevity of life.

It's expected that a person in their teens,

twenties and thirties will exercise to maintain a satisfactory level of fitness. But, I know many persons in their early fifties, sixties and seventies who wake up very early every morning to exercise before going to work. Some are corporate executives, some have blue-collar jobs, but all maintain extremely busy schedules. My company's office is in a building that I share with one other firm. That company employs a man in his sixties who is an active distance runner.

I share my personal experience and the stories of others to emphasize the existence of numerous examples of people of varying age, circumstances, situations and legitimate physical limitations who place a priority on exercise because it's an important part of "taking care of yourself." We could all arguably justify the decision not to exercise regularly, but refuse to do so. What's your excuse not to exercise?

Exercise isn't restricted to physical activity. It also incorporates consistent brain stimulation to hone mental acuity. Mind exercise quickens your ability to grasp, analyze, interpret and remember concepts and data. A sharp mind affords you better critical thinking and conflict resolution skills. Mental stimulation provides an overall rejuvenation for any person.

I engage purposely in three specific daily activities that provide mental stimulation. The first is reading. The English author and poet, Joseph Addison stated, "Reading is to the mind what exercise is to the body." I read, at least, one book per month, almost exclusively books of non-fiction. I'm not speaking out against or "knocking" other genres of books; non-fiction just happens to be my personal preference. Reading plays a very specific role in my life. It offers me an affordable learning opportunity that continually expands my personal boundaries of understanding. It's one of my growth activities of choice. I encourage everyone to read, whatever the genre or medium, to obtain the benefits of this form of mental stimulation. I have always maintained that reading is one of the most educational opportunities that we can provide ourselves. Each page read is another seed planted in the garden of our mind that if watered, and cultivated properly, reaps extraordinary crops of knowledge that will nourish the reader for a lifetime.

My second daily mental stimulation activity is solving crossword and jigsaw puzzles. This exercise provides another tool for mind sharpness. Puzzles challenge me to think, exercise my problem-solving skills, while expanding and reinforcing vocabulary. Despite the challenging nature of puzzles, they also provide a fun and relaxing diversion in the course of my demanding days.

My third daily activity is to gain mental nourishment through an audio format. I listen to a spiritual sermon, lecture (on some educational topic of interest) or a motivational speech or message from a variety of persons that I find educational, inspirational or motivational. This listening may occur in the morning in my home office when I prepare for the day, while driving in my car between appointments or headed to my office, on a plane or train as I frequently travel, or during my pre-bed relaxation mode.

Those activities are what work for me, but may not be your desired choices. However, you must identify and incorporate the right activities into your daily schedule that provide mentally challenging and stimulating opportunities for your brain.

Eat Healthier

My doctor, John F. D'Avella M.D., often tells me, "We dig our graves, one fork bite at a time." That statement is his gentle way of reminding me to stop eating bad foods that have long-term harmful effects on the body. He cautions me that there is no escape from the damage that they cause. I once believed that I could eat any food that I desired (and as much of it as I wanted to) as long as I was willing to exercise hard enough to work off any weight gain. It was my firm but flawed philosophical belief. I was in great physical shape, and I associated health strictly with physical conditioning and the visual manifestation of my perception of physical fitness. But, Dr. D'Avella would always dismiss my philosophy, stating, "It's going to catch up with you one day. Develop good habits now." Now I understand the science of blood chemistry and how the cumulative effect of eating bad foods reflects in your blood work. Many people look great but have a plethora of health issues associated with bad eating habits.

As I've gotten older, I've had to change my eating habits to lower cholesterol levels. My body's metabolism has decreased, and it takes more exercise time to burn off calories than during my younger years. I work three times as hard to obtain the same results as when I was younger. Proper eating habits have become one of my primary strategic preventative tactics to stay healthy.

Developing healthy eating habits lowers the probability of acquiring any number of chronic health diseases such as heart disease, diabetes and cancer significantly. A healthy person does not experience the burden of higher health care costs and medical bills. Obesity issues diminish; causing a person to look better physically, experience higher energy levels and better moods. Eating healthy adds years to your life.

Rest More

I remember visiting a health fair (almost ten years ago) and taking a test entitled, "What's your real age?" The medical booth attendants explained that a person's chronological age doesn't always measure up, and quite often differs from his or her "real" age. The discrepancy pertains to the care that he or she has taken of his or her body. The nurses explained that it is capable for a person to be 30 years of age and due to neglectful eating, exercise regimens, and other habits, have placed 40 years of stress on their body. Likewise, it's also possible that a person in his or her fifties could possess a body that is the functional equivalent of a person in his or her forties. The test was a questionnaire with an extensive list of questions examining numerous categories of individual lifestyle habits. I cruised confidently through the test questions providing truthful answers that I assumed would produce an excellent report of health that compared me to a teenager. To my surprise, I was told that I was five years older than my actual age. Once I accepted the fact that the test wasn't flawed or that I wasn't the victim of some television "gotcha" show, I was ready to listen and hear the truth.

The nurse explained that all of my answers cross-categorically were in line with what they hope to see with their patients in every area but one, rest. The test question that ruined the entire test for me was simply this: How many days of the week do you get eight hours of sleep? My answer fell in the "less than two days per week" range. In fact, I averaged about four to five hours of sleep a night. I was shocked and amazed at the reality that proper eating, exercise, and other lifestyle habits could be sabotaged by missing a few hours of sleep a day. It was an education that I'll never forget.

I learned that the benefits of sleep were similar to most of the benefits of eating healthy and exercising. The body has a strong need for rest. Your body will adjust to the amount of sleep to which you provide it and compensate, as long as you force it to do so. But, it does not eliminate the need for more sleep. There is a direct correlation between sleep and the quality of life that a person experiences. Individuals who average seven to nine hours of sleep per night live longer. Well-rested people have better mental performance, including memory and sharpness. They have better stamina and fatigue less throughout the course of each day. Sleep allows the body to repair itself and build resistance to ailments and injuries. The phrase that my doctor stated about eating is also applicable to rest. "It's going to catch up with you. Develop good habits now."

Taking charge of your life is a bold but necessary step to accomplishing the extraordinary. It may not be easy, but it's within your ability to perform. It's a conscious choice. Choosing to take charge of your life is an awareness of current positioning and a commitment to strive to reach your desired destination. It's preparation for success, a prerequisite for action.

Take Action!

If you have not grasped the concept yet, this chapter is about action. Every preceding chapter in this book has prepared you for this moment. You had to identify and separate yourself from the dream killers in your life, insulate yourself to control your environment, get your mind right, dare to dream and dream big. But all of the learning, preparation, effort, good intention and planning swirl down the drain, lost forever if you don't take action. Are you a talker or a doer? At some point in every race, runners have to run. The starting gun for the race of your life has already gone off. Why are you waiting? Accomplish your dream. Henry Ford said, "You can't build a reputation off of what you're going to do." It takes more than just a decision to dream now. Translate decision into action. Let today be the start of something spectacular. Take hold of the big idea that you dared to dream and set the wheels of action in motion. It's time to execute; get things done!

The English poet Dante Gabriel Rosetti stated, "Look in my face; my name is Might-have-been; I am also called No-more, Too-late, Farewell." This powerful statement summarizes the tragic result that procrastination creates. The potential for greatness will always fall victim to the trap of procrastination. Opportunities pass and potential is neutralized, leaving the idle dreamer with a regretful memory of what might have been. Don't let this statement be the testimony that sums up your life.

CHAPTER SIX
Dream Now!

_____

APPLICATION EXERCISES

_____

1. What current circumstances or situations do you need to change in your life to advance your life?

2. What specific steps are you willing to take to begin the process of change for those items identified in question one.
   a. In the next seven days
   b. Over the next 30

3. Make a list of your goals and then:
   a. Qualify them to ensure that they are "S.M.A.R.T." Are they:
      i. Specific: Provide clear definition of the goal (what and how)?
      ii. Measurable: How will you measure progress towards this goal?
      iii. Attainable: Is it reasonable for you to accomplish this goal?
      iv. Realistic: Is it possible to achieve? Is it feasible?
      v. Timely: When will you accomplish the goal?

4. Set goals for a regular physical exercise regimen:
   a. How many days per week will you commit to exercise?
   b. What specific activities will you do during those days?

5. Set goals for a regular mental exercise regimen:
   a. How many days per week will you commit to exercise?
   b. What specific activities will you do during those days?

Chapter 7: Persist

"Nothing in the world can take the place of Persistence. Talent will not; nothing is more common than the unsuccessful men with talent. Genius will not; unrewarded genius is almost a proverb. Education will not; the world is full of educated derelicts. Persistence and determination alone are omnipotent. The slogan 'Press on' has solved and always will solve the problems of the human race."

- Calvin Coolidge

I have a friend named Greg Jones who often tells me that three facts hold true regarding the concept of dream attainment or the accomplishment of any significant undertaking in life. He says, "It will be harder than you think it'll be, it'll take longer than you think it will take, and it'll cost more than you think it will cost." I found it to be a cool catchphrase upon first hearing. However, the true beauty of its words and the depth of meaning didn't sink in until I heard him declare it a few more times. One day the proverbial light switch turned on. I came to realize that it accurately summarizes the harsh reality of striving to accomplish the extraordinary. I'll translate my interpretation of the statement's meaning.

It Will Be Harder Than You Think!

The pursuit of every dream must begin with the understanding that attainment will be, harder than you think. There is no precise system of measurement that accounts for the exact number of hours, the amount of effort and the degree of sacrifice that is involved in accomplishing the extraordinary. The enormity and complexity of the process that leads to dream attainment is usually underestimated. The difference between assessment and reality is represented by a significant gap. The gap is comprised of many factors including an overestimation of one's own knowledge and abilities, more hurdles experienced than anticipated and more twists and turns along the road to success than predicted. The gap causes frustration levels to fluctuate, often stimulating the desire to give up. But the successful dreamer never gives up, never falling victim to the gap. He or she understands a critical fact that one must internalize.

Success is not a common occurrence but occurs for common people who decide that nothing will separate them from their success and choose to persist until they prove themselves correct. Success doesn't spontaneously happen. Don't waste valuable time hoping that a fluke happenstance will usher you into your destiny. There is no magical elixir. Magic potions are cartoon fantasy. Lucky breaks are not coming your way. In fact, there is no such thing as luck. One must create his or her luck by combining a relentless work ethic; a determination to succeed, a consistency of preparation and the awareness and willingness to seize the opportunities that life presents that offer a bridge from dream to reality.

It Will Take Longer Than You Think It Will Take

Several years ago my children's collection of toys began to hold the family room in our house hostage. My wife and I needed a game plan to enjoy space in our home, less the ever-looming presence of stuffed animals and noise-making electronic toys. We made a bold decision. We would finish our basement. The exciting proposition of a true "man cave" triggered the creativity of a design gene that was unknowingly suppressed deep within my soul. I sketched out an incredible basement blue print to scale that included a bathroom, office area and spare room (for whatever reason we would decide an extra room was needed). I accounted for built in bookcases, storage compartments and a built in television area that would contain the pride of any man cave, a big-screen television with a surround sound stereo system. I envisioned an entertainment arena that would rival any movie theater, shaking the foundations of our house with every bass boom.

The easy part was obtaining quotes from the five contractors that came highly recommended to bring this vision to reality. They all predicted a 30-day time frame to project completion. The tough part was digesting the cost of each of the estimates. Labor was quoted as a whopping 70-90% of the cost of doing the job. I was not aware if that ratio was consistent with industry standard, but it proved to be inconsequential. That cost factor did not sit very well with me, and I refused to pay quoted costs. I had a serious decision to make in regards to the future of my basement.

I made a bold determination after careful thought and consideration. I would finish the basement myself. I thought, why not? I was significantly handy. I had performed my share of "do-it-yourself" home projects over the years as a result of home and rental property ownership. I had done roofing jobs with friends to learn a skill that I thought might be necessary for my house. I had fought many rounds of drywall installation and painting. I had helped co-workers with framing for home additions and basement projects. I didn't consider myself an expert by any means, but I was comfortable with my general knowledge and intelligence level. I was confident in my ability to research, watch videos and figure out any problem that might arise. I wasn't above asking for help if necessary. I even had a few buddies that would help with certain portions of the project. I would hire an electrician for the electrical work. I would hire a plumber for the bathroom and heating components. The rest was an investment of my time and effort.

I am proud to report the successful completion of the project. It was an incredible cost saving. I spent a fraction of the cost to complete the entire project than the cheapest quote obtained during my pricing process that satisfied my frugal nature. The bonus is that my family has a great recreational space. I have a place to relax and detach from the hectic responsibilities that life throws my way, in prime "man space!" In fact, my basement has become a popular destination for Super Bowl, boxing and other sport viewing parties for friends and family. It was a good decision. However, there is a point to this story.

The average time frame that was quoted for project completion by the contract professionals was between 30-45 days. I was aware of my inability to match that time expectation. I factored in a little wiggle room considering the fact that I'm not a professional contractor, nor did not have a team of persons helping each day. I anticipated three to four months to project completion. I was gravely mistaken. The entire process had taken a year before I was comfortably satisfied with the work.

And years after completion, there are still detail items that need attention. Most people would not recognize the majority of those items, but I know. I still have work to do. I won't be entirely satisfied until the finished product matches the image of the dream as originally envisioned. I know that I'll have to commit additional time to make the necessary adjustments. I've learned that no dream is ever complete. Dreams will always require maintenance.

I experienced a barrage of unaccountable factors that consumed time during the process. Trial and error was an example. Often I knew what to do, but the process of doing it the right way had to be learned and mastery came from repetition. I had to demolish improperly constructed work on more than one occasion and rebuild it correctly to obtain and preserve the quality and integrity of my expectation. Confusion and uncertainty arose from time to time. I found myself occasionally unsure of next steps and had to consult and seek the direction necessary to proceed in the appropriate fashion. And there were times when I changed directions entirely; opting to redesign or amend previous design plans to satisfy changing desires.

The takeaway from this story is that it will take longer than you think. It's a safe bet to (at least) double or triple the anticipated time frame that you associate with accomplishing extraordinary dreams. An array of random and unanticipated factors, situations and circumstances that cause delay await any journey upon which you will embark. My basement project was not an overly complicated project, nor was it one that challenged the mental confines of possibility. In fact, the vast majority of people who know me well would probably agree that finishing a basement is a project well within my capability of accomplishment. But I innocently and foolishly estimated a third of the time necessary to accomplish that endeavor. If that simple error was made with regards to something perceived as doable, imagine the effort and time frame required to realize something extraordinary. Prepare yourself to accept a particular set of facts relating to dream attainment; it will be harder than you think it will be and it will (without question) take longer than you think it will take.

It Will Cost More Than You Think It Will Cost

The error in my line of thinking regarding my basement project was attributing cost strictly to financial measures. The monies associated with the project were but one "piece of the pie." There was a host of hidden costs that proved to be more expensive than dollars and cents. Sacrifice is the word that best describes those costs. Devoting hours a day (above and beyond those required for the existing responsibilities of my life) towards a project required an extensive amount of sacrifice. I had to deprive temporarily myself of many wants, needs and personal pleasures in exchange for the prospect of completing my goal. The first sacrifice was time. I lost valuable daily interactive "quality time" with my family. Personal time for thought, reflection, meditation and preparation were also lost. The time and ability to take advantage of social opportunities were lost because being locked into a project has damaging effects on a person's social life. Invitations to social events, gatherings and outings were often declined because devotion to project completion took priority. Picturesque places went unseen, as opportunities to travel could not be seized. Fun took a back seat to commitment, dedication and persistence.

The second sacrifice was the impact on physical and emotional health. The physical and emotional stress associated with planning, initiating and executing any major endeavor has some form of measurable effect on a person's physical and psychological well-being, even if not obviously apparent. Mental fatigue is one manifestation. One might consider throwing in the towel and conceding victory. Stress might present itself as physical discomfort or exhaustion as the process proves strenuous on one's body.

I found the bodily effects of a construction project physically taxing over the course of a year. I believe that some of the occasional aches and pains that I experience to this day are a result of that endeavor. But there were also emotional effects associated with that process. There were plenty of moments where I questioned my decision not to hire a contractor to perform the work. Four months into the project, I realized I had seriously miscalculated the required time frame to completion. At the six-month period, I realized that I was swimming in a proverbial ocean with no sight of the shore. At nine months, I grew angry with myself for allowing my decision-making process to reach the resolution that a "do-it-yourself" project was acceptable. The final three months of the project were simply emotionally painful. I was completely stressed out. It was the proverbial, "light at the end of the tunnel," that allowed me to persevere to completion. However, I was emotionally and physically exhausted for a month after I finished the project. There was a substantial cost to this project that included financial, physical and emotional components. But I made it!

If you haven't caught on yet, the entire point of this story is that persistence is the component critical to accomplishing any effort of significance. Every aspect of planning and preparation can be properly factored. "I's" can be dotted and "T's" can be crossed. A clear road map and detailed blueprint can offer clear vision. However, the will to persist must power you through the pain and discomfort that the process of fulfillment bestows upon the individual who dares to dream. Motivational speaker Les Brown says, "wanting something is not enough. You must hunger for it. Your motivation must be extremely compelling to overcome the obstacles that will invariably come your way." One of the earliest quotes that child athletes learn is, "winners never quit, and quitters never win." Winning will be harder than you think. It will take longer than you think, and will cost more than you think it will cost. Persistence separates those that win from those who simply believe winning is a good idea.

I believe that there are four things that you have to determine to maintain a sufficient level of persistence: Know your what; know your why; know your how; and renew your passion.

Know Your What & Know Your Why!

Mark Twain stated, "the two most important days in your life are, the day you are born, and the day you find out why." I opened this book sharing a personal story of my first encounter (of memory) with a dream killer. I recounted my story as a high school athletic recruit committing to a major collegiate sports program. The choice offered an incredible opportunity for success, but a more challenging road than other options at my disposal. In that story, I was discouraged from pursuing a dream that I believed personally attainable and desirable. In fact, the term, "discouraged," is a kind description at best of the shameless but not unpredictable acts of a dream killer. I was told in blunt fashion that I didn't stand a punchers chance of winning in that endeavor. I was told that I didn't have the ability or capability to succeed in that effort despite my dedication and firm conviction that failure was not an option. The discouragement of that dream killer did not dampen my determination or cripple my commitment to accomplish the goals that I had set for myself. I refused to be deterred. Even at a young age, I was the benefactor of a high level of self-confidence. I understood that dream killers didn't know enough about me to define my possibility. They could never gauge my level of commitment, work ethic or the sacrifices that I was willing to make to be successful in any endeavors in life. But that is **everyone's** reality when facing dream killers, even if they aren't operating at that level of consciousness.

In my recruiting situation, history proved the dream killer wrong. But, a certain consistency exists regarding the dream killer. In competition with a confident, goal setting and persistent dreamer, the dream killer will always lose the battle. The power of a dream killer is, has always been and will always be perceived. The dream killer has been historically effective utilizing tactical deceit and trickery, draining countless numbers of dreamers of the will to thrive in a sustained fashion for generations. The consequences have been a long trail of doubt, disbelief, and determent, resulting in a graveyard of discarded dreams.

My collegiate experience provided four of the most significant years of personal growth and development in my life span. Indiana University afforded more than a classroom education and a bachelor's degree. It offered a series of life experiences unattainable in a classroom setting, which ultimately shaped the foundation of the person that I am today. The cross-country trek from east coast living to a Midwestern city existence provided a sink or swim moment for that period of my life. It was an extremely tough time, one of the greatest challenge periods that I have faced. That seventeen-year-old boy was forced to mature quickly to balance the class schedule of a student with the practice and competition schedule of a collegiate athlete in an atmosphere of unfamiliarity and discomfort. I adopted a champion's mindset in response to adversity, a will to win and an unswerving determination to never give up until victory is obtained. I learned how to work harder than anyone else is willing to work, and endure the pain of the training and preparation process longer than anyone else to position myself for victory. I became a champion, but better than that, I learned how to be a champion. During my four years as an Indiana Hoosier, I learned that excuses are tools of the incompetent and those who use them seldom amount to anything but excuses.

My life would be drastically different if not for my Indiana experience. My collegiate experience was an invaluable, perspective providing, life changing time. But it would have never been my story had I listened to the direction of a dream killer who attempted to swindle me out of my future. I would be a fraction of the person that I have become without that four-year experience. It is because of that encounter with a dream killer, combined with subsequent dream killer encounters, that I discovered my "what." "What" I would do, is devote the rest of my life to educating, inspiring and empowering people to do better, be better and accomplish more than they thought was possible before their interaction with me. My "what" involves encouraging people to dream and inspiring and empowering their ability to accomplish the extraordinary on a daily basis! My "what" consists of depriving the dream killer of control by diverting that power into the hands of those who need it, dreamers! My "what" propels dreamers towards dream attainment.

I hope that my "what" offers you a better understanding of the questions that you need to answer for yourself. What is **your** "what?" What are you going to do that will define your claim as a person of value and significance? What are you going to do that makes a difference, creates an impact or leaves an impressive footprint that represents the quality of your efforts?

It is my unwavering belief that the vast majority of people sell themselves short of their potential and possibilities, mainly due to exposure to a barrage of negative individuals who encourage mediocrity. Combined with a limited association to persons who uplift and inspire, it is not difficult to understand why so many come to be achievement challenged. They ingest the medicine of dream killers that prove to be nothing more than deadly poisons. Dream killer venom has a neurotoxic effect. It attacks the mind, disrupting normal brain function and activity. It disables belief and disassembles dreams. The neurotoxin then attacks the central nervous system. It intercepts the signals sent from the brain to the muscles that communicate action toward the realization of dreams, rendering the dreamer paralyzed. Dream killer venom also has a hemotoxic effect. It weakens the heart muscle. It attacks the cardiovascular system, destroying healthy cells; restricting blood flow until the dreamer is in a state of cardiac arrest, in need of resuscitation to restore life and the will to live according to dreams previously imagined.

I consider myself the anti-venom to dream killer toxin. The personal story that I shared is but one testimony that I offer to prove that anyone can survive a dream killer attack. My "why" is rooted in my personal story. I don't want another person to be discouraged from their pursuit of accomplishing the extraordinary because another's perspective alters his or her belief in self. I don't want another person to accept defeat when victory is attainable. My "why" is a personal conviction that I have a calling to help people obtain a life of success, fulfillment and completeness according to their dreams and expectations for themselves.

There is an important link between my "what" and "why." It's imperative that you understand the relationship between yours. "What" you want to do must be powered by your "why." Accomplishing the extraordinary is never an easy task. As we have established, it will be harder than you think. It will take longer than you think and it will cost more than you think it will cost. The reasons associated with **why** must be your constant motivator. They must provide a continuous supply of fuel that will drive you through difficult times and complicated circumstances. Understanding the "why" provides clarity, aligning purpose with passion. The "why" becomes your proverbial guiding light, capable of navigating you through any nighttime wilderness experience that you'll encounter on your journey.

Understand Your How

It is possible to have a firm handle on what extraordinary feats you want to accomplish and a strong grasp of why you are compelled to achieve them. However, a lack of an understanding of how you'll reach your aspirations leaves you wandering aimlessly with a decreased chance of ever finding your destination. In chapter six we discussed developing a plan. Take a moment to flip back the pages of this book to read that section once again. The ability to persist is greatly assisted with the help of an organized plan, providing a route down which your passion is enabled to drive your purpose.

But having a plan is not enough. You must also **understand** the measurable results that your plan is supposed to yield. A change of plans is a common occurrence. However, the need to change, the timing of that change and reasons that stimulate change are wrapped up in your ability to **understand** when you have reached a critical junction point at which your current plan will not generate the results to satisfy your direction.

Put More Wood on the Fire
- Renew Your Passion

One of my family's favorite wintertime activities is to gather around the fireplace in the family room of our home as the warmth of burning logs and open flames knock the season chill out of the air. We have been known to toast a few marshmallows to sandwich between graham crackers and chocolate squares to make the delectable but devilishly unhealthy treats called, "Smores." Often we watch a family movie while our bare toes soak up the heat waves that radiate from the fireplace. Other times, conversation dominates the family fireplace time. Whatever the chosen fireplace activity, we find it relaxing and enjoyable. However, that's not how the story began. In fact, one would have never imagined that we would have found family contentment around the fireplace after the birth of my daughter. She was once deathly afraid of open flames and wood burning. The unmistakable cracking sound that's produced by burning wood used to scare the living daylights out of her during her toddler years. She would scream at the top of her lungs, cover her ears and run as far away from the family room as possible at the sight of burning wood. This young lady put quite the damper on what had been a source of quality family time for years. We had to shut down the fireplace activity for almost two years.

We're not sure what changed, how it changed or why it changed, but for some reason, things changed. My daughter Logan underwent a complete reversal of position relating to her fear of fire. One wintry day she uttered, "let's build a fire." Imagine the shock and confusion. Should we dare? Were we being set up for a cruel "gotcha" joke? Or had the universe shifted in some strange way, causing the stars to align in our favor? Whatever the case, we had to test the theory. So, we built a fire. That was the first day of the glorious reunion of our family and our fireplace. Now she loves sitting in front of the roaring flames (and often too close for my liking). Her favorite moment is when there is a need to put another log on the fire. She often tells me, "put more wood on the fire." Logan gets excited when fire consumes the new log causing the flames to intensify. She describes this as the moment that wood gets excited. In her mind, every time that wood is added, it renews the passion of the flame, and she gets the opportunity to watch it burn for a longer period of time. When we are ready to let the fire burn out, we inform her that no additional logs will be added to the flames. It's a disappointing time for her. Her response is often, "that's a shame."

I share that story because the fire symbolizes your journey to accomplish anything extraordinary. The flames represent the intensity level of your passion and energy. You will always experience periods of high energy and raging power. But that energy fades over time, as fuel reserves decrease. You have to stoke the fire to keep it going. As my daughter would say, it would be, "a shame" to let your fire burn out. Find a way to maintain excitement about the goals towards which you strive. Renew the passion of your flame on a continuous basis to keep your fire burning hot for longer periods of time. The need to sustain a maximum level of intensity, productiveness or effectiveness requires one simple thing; put more wood on the fire.

The third President of the United States, Thomas Jefferson, penned words in the Declaration of Independence in reference to each individual's inalienable rights that include, "life, liberty, and the pursuit of happiness." Scholars, politicians and other intellectuals have debated the exact meaning of that statement for generations. However, my interpretation offers the belief that any person can dare to dream and be free to engage in the relentless pursuit of that dream to live life in a state of contentment. The individual pursuit of happiness is yours alone. The only person to truly count on for assistance in obtaining a desired state of happiness is the individual who stares back at you from the mirror. You will live out some form or quality of life. You have the liberty to exist, as you desire. But will you truly exercise your inalienable right to pursue that, which makes your life worth living? Putting more wood on the fire is about providing or creating opportunities that continually encourage you to become a person of destiny. Self-motivation is the invaluable skill that must be developed and applied. The ability to persist for significant periods of time or through difficult challenges is dependent upon your ability to generate self-motivation. The most effective way to persist is to create a link between you and your ultimate goal. Envision the life that the achievement of your goal will afford. Draw upon that picture to produce sources of motivation. Allow yourself to experience life as you desire or reward yourself for milestones along the way. If your goal affords you a lifestyle of wealth and material items, embark on a dream-building escapade in which you experience the life that you desire for a day. One of my closest friends often tests drives high-end luxury cars. He can't afford them now, but he is a workaholic whose work ethic is tied to the result that he envisions, a level of wealth that enables his ability to drive these types of cars. An occasional test drive centers his focus, re-aligning his target direction. It restores his passion. It's his way of putting wood on the fire when his flame gets low.

Perhaps your goal is more personal in nature. I'm reminded of a guy in an airport lounge that (initially) engaged me in sports conversation as we watched sports highlights on one of the televisions mounted on the lounge walls. The conversation transitioned from sports to health as we joked about our aging bodies, not being as young as we once were and unable to make many of the plays featured on the highlight reel. He was slightly overweight and shared his motivated journey to lose an additional 50 pounds. He communicated his struggles with obesity throughout the duration of his life, experiencing extreme weight fluctuations. He battled high blood pressure, high cholesterol and other health issues relating to obesity. A cardiac event almost ended his life a few years' before our conversation, sparking a series of major changes in his life. He vowed to take charge of his life and was proud of the fact that his efforts to date resulted in a weight loss of over 100 pounds in a two-year period. He was now two-thirds of the way towards his goal. What I found particularly interesting is the "wood" that he chose to put on his fire. He showed me a picture contained on his phone that a family member had taken of him laying on his hospital bed in the hours immediately following his heart attack. He was connected to an assortment of tubes and monitors as he fought for his life. The photograph that he keeps provides a visual representation of how close he came to death due to chronic self-neglect. He shared that he kept a copy on his refrigerator to deter unhealthy eating. The picture was also motivation to maintain a consistent exercise regimen. He stated that he glances at it anytime he needs motivation to "stay the course" during his weight loss journey. It was his way to renew his passion. It was his wood on the fire. What will be yours? What kind of wood will you throw on your fire?

CHAPTER SEVEN
Persist!

APPLICATION EXERCISES

1. What is your "what?"
   a. What are you going to do that offers your desired level of success and significance?
   b. How are you going to be different than the average person?
2. What is your "why?"
   a. Why are you motivated to accomplish your "what?"
   b. How will your "why" provide continual inspiration to carry you through the rough process to accomplish your "what?"
3. Understand your how
   a. How are you going to accomplish your "what?"
      i. What are the steps to accomplishment?
   b. What measureable results should your plan yield at each step?
4. Put more wood on the fire
   a. What activities will constitute putting more wood on the fire so that your passion continues to burn strong?

8

Chapter 8   Empower Others

"Whatever we accomplish belongs to our entire group, a tribute to our combined effort."

- Walt Disney

The English playwright John Heywood is credited for the popular adage, "Rome was not built in a day, but they were laying bricks every hour." This two-part quote is a powerful marriage of two statements of equal significance and value, strategically linked to prove a larger point. "Rome was not built in a day" is the portion of that saying often quoted to reference the need to allot proper time to complete a desired task of significance or reach an anticipated achievement of impressive magnitude. It's a reminder that greatness isn't attained easily nor should immediate success be expected when undertaking large endeavors. It's a plea for patience and a warning against rashness to ensure that a quality product emerges as the fruit of one's labor. It's a perfect lead-in to the second part and what I view as the more noteworthy part of the adage.

"But they were laying bricks every hour" speaks to the laborious process that it took to build Rome. The building of Rome required a steady, consistent, hourly and brick-by-brick construction process with daily repetition over a span of years. It was a routine that required endurance and perseverance. Rome (as the reference pertains to) is the visual manifestation of that brick laying process. However, I find the most interesting and powerful part of that adage to be the word, "they." Let me explain!

Most scholars would agree that history characterizes Rome as one of greatest civilizations of all times. The Roman influence is evident in various components of modern culture across the globe in areas such as law, government, science, art, philosophy and military discipline. Rome remains a popular destination where tourists flock for a glimpse of the ancient ruins that represent the magnificence of what was once, the Roman Empire. I struggle to find words that adequately describe my personal experience in Rome. I loved the food, enjoyed the people and was fascinated by the historical backdrop of the ancient city. I found monumental structures such as, the Colosseum, the

Roman Forum, Trevi Fountain, Pantheon, St Peters Basilica, Vatican City and the Spanish Steps of Rome particularly fascinating. I was amazed by the intricate design and detail work of each, and marveled at the enormity of their build. My exploration of the city elicited the same question repeatedly; how did they build such a collection of great structures? The technological advances of Roman architecture are legendary, but despite the complexity of construction, and the enormous thought, time and planning that must have defined the process, the answer remained quite simple. Everything was built one brick at a time. An emperor commissioned every structure in ancient Rome. An architect is credited to every design. But who laid the bricks? It was "they!" And, "they" laid the bricks every hour, daily, for years.

Who are "they?" "They" are the persons, the workers and the soldiers in the trenches willing to fight with you and for you until victory is won. "They" are the forceful movement of people; the help that you will need to assemble and empower to be effective and efficient. "They" represent the collective effort of everyone necessary to bring a dream or vision to reality. "They," were necessary to build Rome, and are critical to the completion of whatever extraordinary creation that you dare to dream. Go find, assemble and empower them!

Empowering others grants authorization to persons for the performance of duties that you might have them carry out on your behalf. Empowering others helps them realize their full potential by providing growth opportunities and experiences that allow them to blossom and flourish. It is an understanding that their success leads to yours. Empowering others involves sharing information, delegating responsibility and trusting the competency and decision-making ability of those empowered, by providing them the latitude and flexibility (within a structured framework) to exercise their own expertise in working toward the fulfillment of the established goal. Empowering others allows you to leverage the brainpower, talents, abilities and capabilities of a group of qualified and dedicated persons whose involvement and participation will accelerate the materialization of your dream. Empowering others requires you to, "let go" in order to grow. By releasing the notion that the quality of your individual efforts outweighs the collective benefit of a group attempt, you multiply effectiveness producing a better result than previously imagined. Empowering others involves three steps.

1. Lead

The quest to accomplish the extraordinary is a complicated endeavor. However, if the effort is successful in bearing fruit, it will provide tremendous personal benefits or produce incredible societal impact or both. Regardless of the intent or the eventual outcome, you'll have to spearhead the effort. It's your dream, your vision, thus your responsibility to lead. Dreaming bears a significant and unavoidable level of leadership responsibility regardless of your feelings surrounding that truth or level of comfort assuming that duty. If you're going to engage, involve and have expectations of those whom you empower, then you better lead them or be willing to travel to a destination of their choice and settle with their view of your vision of paradise. Apply these four principles as you lead.

Lead with purpose!

Define, develop and cast a vision. A leader without purpose will quickly lose credibility with their followers. In the absence of direction, people seek their own path. They tune out the sound of your music and march to the beat of their own drummer. Their unguided path will lead to a destination of conflict and controversy. Provide a clear, concise and compelling purpose that excites the mind and captures the heart of those who will follow your leadership. Purpose is the glue that will bind and motivate your team around a shared goal. It's the "why" that we explored in chapter seven of this book. Clarity of purpose aligns effort toward expectation, channeling energy to its most productive form. A concise vision offers a simple non-complicated understanding of direction. It is easy to grasp and remember; thus, a source of continual focus and reinforcement. The steps involved in bringing vision to reality may prove complicated, but understanding the vision should never be. A compelling vision motivates your followers. It pulls them into the narrative of your story, creating a sense of placement, ownership and responsibility for the cause. It creates buy-in. The compelling nature of your vision is what will stimulate movement, transitioning thought to action and ultimately, accomplishment.

Lead with Confidence

We discussed the subject of confidence briefly in chapter three. I defined confidence as the belief in your own abilities and capabilities and discussed the energizing effect that it has on your life. It should be no surprise that confidence is a powerful trait of great leaders and will be a necessary tool in your leadership toolbox. Confidence allows you to lead more effectively and efficiently by providing a variety of benefits. A strong sense of self-confidence empowers sound decision-making to make the bold and tough decisions that leaders must perform with a high degree of poise, even if those choices are risky or unpopular. A confident leader naturally commands the respect of his or her followers and offers a continued sense of reassurance to those persons. Confidence allows a leader to tackle his or her fears, or press through them despite the challenges they pose. A confident leader can be humble. Humility allows a leader to encourage frank, difficult and constructive conversations. It also allows him or her to listen attentively as those discussions take place so the input of the team is valued (and infused as necessary) to increase performance and productivity. A confident leader also understands that a very important goal in leadership is to develop those persons whom he or she has the privilege of leading towards measured growth and increased effectiveness.

Lead with compassion

The 26th President of the United States, Theodore Roosevelt declared, "People don't care how much you know until they know how much you care." This statement captures the relationship building side of leadership. People work harder for those, with whom they connect, identify or who stimulates good feelings. As you lead, continue to highlight and reinforce the value that you have for your followers. Demonstrate your appreciation in a variety of ways. Treat people with respect, fairness, understanding and dignity. Acts of compassion create personal connections in a cognitive, emotional and relational manner. Relationship bonds continue to develop and strengthen when leaders foster environments of empathy, trust and support.

Lead by example

Lead with the courage and conviction that attracts persons to follow. Exemplify a standard of excellence that others will aspire to emulate. Work hard to inspire your people. The trust, confidence and loyalty of your followers is earned and sustained by the personal commitment and work ethic that you display. Conduct yourself as if eyes are watching you at all times because they probably are. Live the standard that you preach. Follow your own rules. Honor the commitments and fulfill the promises that you make. Those acts establish credibility. Don't ask anyone to do something that you've never done or wouldn't do yourself. Exercise integrity at all times.

2. Build the Right Team

In the course of leading multiple basketball teams to 11 National Basketball Association (NBA) championship trophies in total, Phil Jackson attained iconic status and is recorded in sports history as one of the greatest coaches to pace an athletic sideline. His 11 titles sit him atop an impressive list of coaches that have won multiple professional sports championships. His coaching style featured the "triangle offense," a complex but extremely effective system that empowered players to read situations and react accordingly, offering a wide range of latitude in regards to game play decision-making. Successful execution required highly engaged, high-performance, high-energy and constant-movement teams committed to effective teamwork.

Many principled ideologies defined Coach Jackson's tenure of coaching, but none more foundational than his approach to assembling talent. Phil said, "The strength of the team is each individual member. The strength of each member is the team." He built teams of persons that would coalesce around a shared philosophy of collective accomplishment. He selected players with the intellectual capacity to see his vision, comprehend his strategy and assimilate into the culture of winning that he created. He acquired players with the physical ability to perform and the specialized skill sets critical to the needs of his formula for success.

I realize that you're not an NBA coach, and will not be building a roster to make a run for an NBA championship. However, you are mounting a championship effort toward success. Empowering others first requires a strategically assembled team. The team you build requires persons who fit into two categories: those who support your vision and those who are qualified to carry it out.

Building the right team begins by assembling people who actually support your vision, values and goals. Each person you add to your team will either help or hurt the cause. Seek individuals that align with your vision and the culture that you create. A person who stands in conflict fundamentally with your philosophy or intended direction will never make the emotional investment, commitment or physical effort that is necessary to satisfy your expectations or needs. His or her lacks of passion will never champion your purpose and produce an undercurrent of negativity capable of sabotaging your entire effort. That negativity can manifest itself in various forms. Morale issues arise from the negative influence of a deterred mind. Productivity suffers. A financial impact is certain, but an opportunity cost exists as well. The opportunity to have the right person in place is missed, depriving you of the production and accomplishment, which could have been gained. The wrong person can also impact the integrity of your cause by damaging the reputation of excellence that you establish. In other words, your brand suffers.

The persons that you empower must be qualified to carry out your vision. A collection of persons supportive of your vision is of no value if they don't possess the ability to bring it to reality. I've developed a simple rule when building teams of persons qualified to carrying out a vision. Each individual added to the team must be a person of "character, competence and commitment." You can't settle with one or two of these traits. Each person must possess all.

Character

Character is the collection of traits and qualities that define a person. They guide a person's thoughts, responses and reactions to every situation and circumstance. Character is the most important factor in my evaluation process when assembling teams of persons who will work with me in any capacity. I must be able to trust that a person will think, speak, make decisions and conduct themself on my behalf in alignment with high moral values and an unquestionable and unwavering ethical standard of operation. They must be a team player, have the right attitude and be coachable. I believe that one can always find a person who is competent to fill a role or perform a task. Demonstrated competence and commitment can be verified through a list of references that any candidate can provide who can speak to a record of performance and drive. However, character is more complicated. It's harder to evaluate. References aren't always reliable as it relates to character. Employers are more than willing to rid themselves of a bad character headache by passing it on to you. I also find it hard to trust that a stranger will evaluate character with the same stringent standard that my scale dictates. Despite the difficult nature, finding persons of character is of critical importance. Competence and commitment without character is a dangerous combination. Empowering people is necessary, but remember one fact. Persons of integrity must be on the front lines to engage the people, conditions and opportunities that your effort will encounter. It will determine your success or failure.

Competence

Competence put simply, is the ability to do what needs to be done. You must determine if a person's skill sets, relevant experience, work ethic and pertinent education and certifications qualify them to perform the role(s) that you seek to fill. It's not overly complicated. They either do or they don't! Competent people get things done consistently

143

through an application of cognitive understanding, physical ability and a sense of pride in the delivery and execution of work according to standards representative of their sense of worth. They bring a level of functionality and dependability to situations in which they are involved, and are necessary to your team's success.

<u>Commitment</u>

Committed people are those who demonstrate a dedication toward your cause and exhibit an energy and enthusiasm toward sustained involvement and accomplishment. Commitment reflects a sense of personal and emotional attachment and loyalty, validated by a consistent willingness to perform in a manner above and beyond what is asked or expected. These highly motivated individuals exhibit initiative, generate momentum and ultimately move your effort toward successful completion in accordance with established goals and objectives.

Another important component of building the right team involves establishing the correct structure and oversight. In other words, each person must understand his or her respective role and responsibilities. Empowering others requires the clear explanation of expectations so that roles are well defined and the efforts of all involved can be focused to set and meet performance goals successfully.

3. Let Them Play

After you have assembled the team and given them a game plan, you have to let them play. You must trust in their ability to perform the duties for which you selected and trained them. Avoid the trap of micromanaging their efforts. Andrew Carnegie once stated that teamwork, "is the fuel that allows common people to attain uncommon results." Micromanagement erodes effective teamwork by destroying trust. It creates frustration and resentment, limiting the potential of the group and the resulting possibilities of their collective effort. Coach, instruct and guide them but give them the opportunity to make decisions and create plays on their own. Encourage them to be their best.

Chapter 9: Inspire Others

"If your actions inspire others to dream more, learn more, do more and become more, you are a leader."

- John Quincy Adams

Have you ever enjoyed a chance meeting with a person from which, the interaction stamped an unforgettable impression on your heart and mind? Have you ever experienced a mind-blowing encounter with a person, which transformed your entire outlook on life, sparking change and altering your life for the better? Have you ever had a conversation or series of talks with someone, during which you gained clarity, a renewed focus or a new perspective on your existence? Have you ever witnessed the astonishing works of someone or participated in an event where a speaker, teacher or trainer left you awestruck, amazed or excited to the point where you could never settle being the same person that you were before that happenstance? Has the career track of anyone ever served as the standard of excellence that you wanted to emulate? Have the efforts, actions or deeds of someone you knew that overcame tremendous odds to succeed ever stimulated the belief that you too could accomplish the extraordinary? Have you ever simply known somebody who makes you feel better about yourself or for whom you strive to be the best person possible?

If you answered, "yes" to any of the above-listed questions, then you have been inspired in some capacity by someone or something. If you have ever reached personal goals or accomplished anything of significance, you have certainly leveraged the power of inspiration. Sources of inspiration can be limitless. They can be elusive or right at your fingertips. They can be spontaneous, unexpected or unexplainable. You can find inspiration, or it can find you, but whatever or wherever it is, it's needed. Inspiration is a seed of motivation. When planted properly, it germinates and takes root, growing with speed and fury blossoming into a beautiful flower of promise. It awakens one's senses to reveal new possibilities and allows a person to overlook or dismiss limitations that previously held him or her bound. It's an invigorating breath of fresh air that revitalizes the soul and gives a new lease on life. Inspiration is what transitions ordinary people and average accomplishments into a state of extraordinary existence.

History chronicles numerous stories of inspiration, of extraordinary feats made possible through the motivated performances of men and women. There are a plethora of historical figures that serve as powerful examples, that despite what people think of you, despite how they feel about you, and despite the barrage of adverse situations and circumstances that life may throw your way, anything is possible. In the face of animosity, discrimination, exclusion or sabotage, inspiration can serve as the great equalizer that overcomes obstacles, alters outcomes and makes victory possible despite overwhelming odds.

History also offers countless examples of persons who have died (in a literal sense) so that you might have the opportunity to live, dream and experience life in the fashion that you desire. Regardless of your race, creed, color or national origin, there are many stories of a people (with whom you can identify) that have struggled, suffered and endured unimaginable hostilities of their time to give you a better opportunity to become the person that you are capable of being. Military personnel have fought to establish, preserve and protect the land in which you reside. Civil Rights figures have fought for the rights that you enjoy today. Trailblazers have pioneered paths in a multitude of disciplines to establish a roadmap and offer a route of travel and hope for the future. Those inspiring truths, accomplishments and sacrifices should trigger a sense of responsibility to carry the generational banner of greatness reflective in your respective history and heritage. It should eliminate any excuse making that stands between you and achievement in whatever field of human endeavor that you choose to pursue.

Inspiration is an important driver towards your success. You should have a good grip on that fact by now. However, striving to accomplish the extraordinary includes providing inspiration to others to drive them towards their desired level of accomplishment, just as others have provided that inspiration for you. Being extraordinary bears the responsibility of helping others see the best within, believe the best about their potential and be the best that they can be. There is no way to gauge accurately the broad range of persons who you might inspire. There is no way to know how an act, conversation or accomplishment might energize another. But, as your successes mount, you will be presented with several opportunities to inspire others. Be ready to fuel the fires of those who need the incentive to burn hotter and brighter. It's a humbling experience to hear stories told of how a small act on your part had a major life-changing impact on someone else's existence. Seize those opportunities to make a difference. The risk is minor; the rewards are high, and the payback is extraordinary. Here's how you do it.

Be Yourself

Rhythm and blues music recording artist Alexander O'Neal released a song entitled, "Fake" in the late 1980's. I may be dating myself with this analogy, as I used to party to this song during my college years, but it serves a purpose. If you're not familiar, an Internet search will provide a tickling listening experience. "Fake" was a hit song played frequently and blared loudly from the speakers that would power the dance or house parties that were typical weekend social events of those times. The song chronicled the artist's early dating history with a woman with whom he had taken a liking. His attraction and fascination quickly faded away after realizing that she was not the person whom he initially believed her to be. In fact, the more time spent together, the more he realized that every aspect of her being was fictitious, including her name, hair, eye color and eyelashes. She was living a fake existence, taking on the appearance and personality of a person that she thought was desirable to others instead of simply being herself. Because of that, he lost interest, respect and ultimately a desire to continue his relationship and association.

The English writer Charles Caleb Colton stated, "Imitation is the best form of flattery." The quote suggests that a person is being complimented when others attempt to imitate their various deeds or actions. There is a natural inclination to emulate powerful examples of accomplishment. People want to be like or attain a similar success of those persons from whom they gain inspiration. There is nothing wrong with that notion. But, imitation must have its limits. Never allow yourself to compromise the integrity of self, seeking to be someone or something that you are not. Never cross the line into the area of impersonation. Imitation is different from impersonation. Impersonation is the act of trying to be someone else, intentionally. The police have a term for it; it's called identity theft. Identity theft is a felony charge of fraud punishable by several years of imprisonment. People aren't impressed and not inspired by a cheap copycat. In fact, being exposed as a fake will destroy the reputation and credibility essential to extraordinary accomplishment. Don't waste time trying to be someone or something that you're not, operating outside of the guidelines and brilliance of your true being. Be yourself. Be genuine. Allow glimpses into the window of your soul to reveal that your thoughts, insights, values and perspectives are indeed your own. Let honesty and sincerity be your calling card. Provide a pathway for people to appreciate the real you. The opportunity to inspire others is gained when you comfortably and confidently embrace and embody your true identity, despite the flaws or faults that may exist. No one is perfect. The ability to achieve success despite individual imperfections provides the narrative for inspiration. Be the best person that you can possibly be, not a bad impersonation of someone else.

Let Your Work Speak For Itself.

There is a gospel hymn that we would sing during my childhood years in church, originally written by The Consolers entitled, "May the work I've done speak for me." The songwriter pens the words from the perspective of a person who is reflective of his or her life. One final wish is requested to be honored after death; let works that have been performed over the course of a lifetime combined with the quality of life that was lived speak to the person resting in the grave. Instead of verbalizing words that boast and brags, let a record of success and accomplishments do all the talking that needs to be done.

Doers, not talkers, inspire people. Which one are you? There is a time for self-promotion. There is a time for others to sing your praises. Strategic marketing provides certain benefits and advantages with respect to advancing your cause or efforts. But, that's a different subject matter than inspiring others, although any marketing effort (by you or for you) should be based on a factual body of work. Talkers waste their time talking about who they are and what they are going to do, in a manner that exhausts all of the productive time needed actually to accomplish anything of value. Doers aren't trying to impress or prove anything to anyone. They don't brag and boast. They are confidant in who they are, in what they are trying to do, and are "laser-focused" on harvesting the desired fruit of their dedicated labor. What are you going to do that will inspire others?

"May the work I've done speak for me," is one of my favorite hymns because its relevancy remains current despite the advanced age of the song. Its message echoes two old adages, "actions speak louder than words" and "the proof is in the pudding." Everyone talks a great game and will portray him or herself in a positive light when given the opportunity. But, individual actions often contradict spoken words, highlighting the contrast between a proven body of work and all good intentions, embellishments or blatant lies. A legacy of living should brag and boast so loudly that words should not be necessary to express the obvious to anyone who is familiar with the person in question. My appeal to you is to live your life in a manner that sets the example. Be an inspiration.

Mentor Someone

My mentor once explained to me that the payment for being mentored is to mentor someone else. The valuable nuggets of wisdom acquired skill and know-how that successful people accumulate must not be hoarded. Just as you have benefitted from the experience of others, your duty is to share that knowledge with others through mentoring after it has afforded you success. Those that mentor embrace the responsibility and appreciate the opportunity to stretch the limits of other persons. Mentoring creates a clear channel for learning, a foundation of support, a framework for continued growth and a pathway to possibilities unattainable without it. Help somebody succeed.

We have explored the benefits associated with being mentored. There should be no doubt or question that taking someone under your wing contributes to his or her overall development and advancement. However, we should not overlook the advantages that mentors receive. Mentoring is a two-way street. It offers a mutually beneficial connection between mentor and mentee, providing immeasurable value to both sides. Let's take a few moments to appreciate the host of rewards that mentoring affords.

You Learn Too!

Mentors typically select and devote their time to persons of sharp mental acuity that possess the potential to be extraordinary. Mentoring provides ongoing interaction with upcoming, educated and energetic individuals with fresh perspectives on life and an overwhelming desire to achieve. What they lack in experience, they make up for in promise. Mentees are smart, energetic and ready to learn and transfer knowledge into productive action. They may represent a different demographic, generation or circle of association than those persons with whom you typically mix. They're savvy in ways, which you are not and offer insights into new trends and methodologies.

Exposure to these types of individuals provides a view of the world through different color glasses and a connection to a realm not typically accessed during a mentor's daily routine. Mentoring provides educational opportunities from which the mentor learns to connect, coach and relate to a variety of persons. He or she acquires skills and stimulates their own personal growth. For example, I have learned (and continue to learn) more about technological trends and gain functional mastery of social media, analytics, computing and mobile device and gadget usage from some of my personal mentees than from any other source at my disposal. In fact, I've gained a healthy level of comfort and have no shame about calling one of them when faced with uncertainty or confusion about one of those areas. I can argue that I learn just as much (in general) from those persons who seek mentoring from me. I've learned that a mentee keeps you current and relevant.

You Gain A Personal Sense of Fulfillment

Mentoring requires a strong investment of time and energy. Stretching the limits of one's imagination, while developing their professional proficiency and building their functional capacity is not a quick process. However, as you share knowledge, experience and acquired skill over time, you instill in others the will, wisdom and resilience to climb proverbial mountains and stand victorious at the top. The beauty of that truth is two-fold.

First, you share in that mountain top experience because you have been an important navigational companion along their journey to accomplishing the extraordinary. Secondly, you receive the blessing of knowing that your involvement, impact and influence were the essential contributing factors to that success story.

As an avid sports fan and self-admitted sports junkie, any television watching opportunity that I am able to seize usually results in the viewing of a sports news channel or collegiate or professional athletic game. I love the thrill of competition, the test of wills and the fact that someone always stands victorious in the end. But one thing tugs at my heartstrings more than any other occurrence during a televised game. I smile whenever the camera scans the crowd to focus in on the parents of someone who has just scored or made a terrific play. I love the excitement and enthusiasm by those who beam with pride as they watch the efforts of their offspring. On the surface, we attribute the excessive jubilation as nothing more than parental praise and pride. However, that joy represents an underlying story. It reflects the hours, days, months and years that they have invested to develop that level of talent on display for the world to enjoy. Those instances of jubilation coupled with the opportunity to celebrate and appreciate moments such as those provide sufficient payment for every sacrifice made so that their child might succeed.

The personal sense of fulfillment that comes from mentoring and inspiring others draws certain parallels to that analogy. Moments of pride, pleasure and satisfaction will result as your influence produces inspired performances from those in whom you invest your time. You'll be cheering loudly, "slapping hands," and throwing "high-fives" with the crowds around you, who have gathered to celebrate the person that you helped raise through mentoring. Don't rob yourself of the opportunity to experience that gratification.

You Build Relationships

The importance of relationship building can never be understated. The ability to form, develop and maintain interpersonal relationships is one of the most critical skills that one can possess. The process of interacting with people is integrated into every facet of our daily lives. We choose to either embrace that process or blow golden opportunities to connect with others on a level that is mutually enriching. Whether you lead a corporate work team, chair a civic fundraising event or offer service through community volunteerism, the quality of personal relationships will make or break your efforts. Establishing healthy relationships is the key to productivity with people and, productivity with people is the key to getting things done in extraordinary fashion. Learning to meet, greet, engage, listen, communicate, captivate, cultivate and motivate people individually and collectively will multiply your probability of success. True appreciation for people and the mutual willingness to assist each other beneficially is linked to the quality of relationship that exists. This holds true regardless of whether one deals with a friend, family member, neighbor, work colleague, civic associate, church member, bus driver, cashier at a store that you frequent or the waitress at a favorite restaurant. People respond favorably for those whom they like and feel a genuine connectedness. They are willing to make exceptions, offer sacrifice and give freely for a person who they trust would do the same for them or would sincerely appreciate the effort. If you don't believe me, then consider the following question: Name a person for whom you'd be willing to get out of bed at 2:00 AM to help change a flat tire in the pouring rain? Or better yet, whose call would you even pick up at 2:00 AM? Here's another scenario. Imagine a request to help someone pack boxes in his or her old home and then assist with the move to a new home (an hour away) on a Saturday morning after you have experienced a rough week at work? Which names listed in the contacts tab of your phone would you help in those situations? Envision this final scenario. A co-worker has a tree fall on their house and asks if they can stay with you for a couple of weeks until his or her roof is repaired. To who would you allow residency in your home? I can assure you that the names produced as answers to any of those questions will be based primarily on the quality and depth of established and existing relationships.

The types of relationships that you have may vary, but one fact will always remain consistent.

159

Any relationship that you hold is valuable and must be appreciated and fostered. The ability to rally large support, move mountains and accomplish the extraordinary through the eager cooperation of people is tied to your capacity to build and preserve healthy relationships.

The greatest reward obtained from mentoring is relationship building. Mentors take on the role of a big brother or sister, aunt or uncle and sometimes a father or mother role in the lives of those whom they advise, but without the stress or overbearing perception that such an authoritative association holds. Regardless of the role, special bonds are built, and life-long friendships develop between mentor and mentee as the continued process of love, support, guidance, inspiration and empowerment take place. The impact of mentoring extends far beyond the time parameter of your mentor-mentee affiliation. The relationship building process that occurs through mentoring allows the mentor to groom future allies, advocates, people of influence and potential partners.

You Leave A Legacy!

The by-product of relationship building is the final benefit of mentoring: building a legacy. The ancient Greek leader Pericles stated, "What you leave behind is not what is engraved in stone monuments, but what is woven into the lives of others." Mentoring provides the needle and thread that weaves an intricately detailed fabric that can be passed down throughout history. The Greek philosopher Socrates mentored and inspired Plato. He in return mentored and inspired Aristotle, outlining a chain of mentoring that left the greatest historical footprint on the subject of philosophy and had the most significant influence on modern thought. Aristotle went on to mentor Alexander the Great, arguably history's greatest military leader. This illustration highlights the power of mentoring and its lasting legacy. The knowledge and influence of a mentor transfers to the mentee, becoming a foundational platform and catalyst for a cycle of new ideas, advancements and achievements that will impact generations to come. As you strive to be a significant person in history, whom will you mentor? Who will be great because of your influence? What great acts will occur because of your inspiration? How will your legacy live on beyond your lifespan?

10

Chapter 10: Accomplish the Extraordinary

"A dreamer is one who can only find his way by moonlight, and his punishment is that he sees the dawn before the rest of the world."
- Oscar Wilde

Life can change dramatically in the blink of an eye. One shocking phone call, tragic misstep or strange twist of fate can provide a significantly different outcome than what you had envisioned for the current day and possibly the rest of your life. I remember sitting in a room with three co-workers on the fourth floor of a building enjoying what we considered a brief but much needed work break. The stress of the day created a level of exhaustion from which we needed a temporary escape. We started discussing our evening plans, eagerly anticipating the fun awaiting us at our respective destinations. We were physically present in the workplace but mentally clocked out despite the few hours of company time that continued to tick by slowly on the clock. The enjoyment of our conversation provided a level of satisfaction and distraction that veiled us to the reality of the situation that was developing. We were insulated in a world of temporary bliss. That's when everything changed.

Without warning, the room filled with smoke and laughter turned to anxiety, as we all understood the blatantly obvious; there was a fire somewhere in the building. Ironically, none of us panicked. We felt somewhat prepared for this event. We had just spent the previous week participating in departmental fire safety and prevention training. We learned how a fire could completely engulf a structure in smoke and flames within four minutes of ignition. We also learned that a fire could produce room temperatures of 2000 degrees. That explained the rapid rate of thick smoke that hurried our way and the increasing level of heat that we began experiencing. Our goal became simple; get out of the building.

We made an immediate dive towards the floor because, in the event of fire, you're supposed to find a low position and crawl out of a smoke-filled room. Despite heavy smoke conditions, there is still usually a foot or two of breathable air, some visibility and cooler temperatures near the floor.

Survival chances increase substantially by staying low and continuing to crawl in those situations. One person kept a hand on the wall to prevent loss of orientation in the darkness as we crawled, searching for the room's exit. The four of us formed a human chain as we made our way out into the hallway. Smoke hampered visibility, so we communicated verbally. In fact, we screamed out to each other frequently to ensure that everyone was doing well in the midst of this crisis. We were confident in our ability to escape but were more concerned about the inability of others who may lie frozen out of fear or might have succumbed to smoke inhalation due to the poor conditions that we were experiencing. We attempted to perform a quick search, crawling around briefly through each room that we passed, ensuring that no one was trapped. We maintained our human chain as we searched, nervous that one of us might get lost during the process. Our attempts to play hero were fruitless as we found no others trapped on our building floor. The temperature in the building was increasing steadily. It was time for us to get out. As we reached an exit on one side of the building floor, we learned a disturbing fact. The exit was blocked, and we needed to find another way out. As we looked back down the hallway from whence we came, it was a dark and intimidating view. The thick smoke had banked down almost entirely to the floor eliminating visibility. We had no breathing equipment, no fire extinguishers or anything else but the clothes on our back. In a moment of temporary paralysis, we all shared the same chilling thought and understood the reality of the situation. There was no other option. We had to go back down that ominous hallway to find another way out.

It's hard to summarize the feelings of disappointment, anger, fear and frustration that we experienced at that moment. We couldn't help but question our own mortality. Is this the place and manner in which we would die? Would all of our hopes and dreams disappear into the plumes of smoke that threatened to choke the life out of us? How tragic an ending would this be to a group of lives with so much promise and potential? We refused to let that happen; we would not give up. Falling victim to this environment and feeding into any feelings of despair was not an acceptable option. We had too much to live for and realized it. We would find a way. That was the end of our brief pity party. We refocused and redirected to tackling the issue at hand, making our way back down the hallway that stood between our survival and us.

Stay low and keep crawling was our strategy. Despite the heat, smoke conditions, fears, obstacles and all other hindrances, we remained determined. We eventually made it to the other end of the hallway and found a different means of egress. Persistence was the key! We descended four flights of stairs, making our way out of the side doors of the building. We all collapsed on the hard pavement, exhausted, coughing, panting and gasping for air. But, we made it! What was, in reality less than a ten-minute ordeal, seemed like it lasted for hours.

As I lay on the ground thankful for the fresh air that was starting to circulate throughout my lungs, I recall feeling a presence standing over me, followed by the sound of an incredibly deep, raspy and chilling voice that said, "Good job McMikle, well done!" But I couldn't see who uttered the words. My eyes, still burning from the smoke, had yet to adjust to the brightness of daylight. A level of confusion and horror replaced my feeling of accomplishment. Maybe I didn't live. Was I in heaven? In response, I uttered one a simple one-word question, "God?" That voice started coughing and then answered my question with another one-word question, "McMikle?" It was hard to classify if the cough was a smoker's cough or that of a sick person or a cross between the two. Either way, I found it unsettling. I responded: "God, do you have a cold, or are you a smoker?" "How is either one possible?" My image of a perfect God was shattered. The initial encounter with my Maker was shaping up to be a dramatically different experience than I anticipated. The voice then responded, "Stop screwing around McMikle and get your butt ready for your next evolution!" It was a startling snap back to the reality of where we were and what were doing.

I began this story purposely omitting the fact that I'm a retired career firefighter. This true story documents my first evolution of "live-burn training," in the fire academy. The exercise was our initial exposure to the reality of fire conditions and an interactive lesson on smoke behavior. It was a powerful visualization of how heated gasses rise, leaving a pocket of breathable air near the floor. Even as smoke banks down off the ceiling towards the floor, there is usually plenty of air offering sufficient time to complete tasks or make an escape as situations warrant. An exercise objective was to learn how to survive and escape without the benefit of breathing apparatus or many of the other tools of survival that firefighters often rely on in the event that their functionality is lost during operation. The evolution also taught us to remain calm and find comfort in hazardous situations, to recognize changing conditions and develop the proficiency to create favorable outcomes despite the challenges or perceived impossibility.

The value of many of the stories and resulting lessons learned during my time "on the job" as a firefighter is priceless. Staring death in the eye on a daily basis offers interesting perspectives on life, decision-making, survival and accomplishment. This evolution was the first of hundreds of training scenarios during a several month stint in the fire academy. It was an intense introduction and overview of each potential workday that I would experience over the next two decades before hanging up my helmet and "turnout gear" in exchange for a career inspiring and empowering lives. It was an overwhelming experience at the time. However, upon reflection, I learned several important life lessons from that situation that applies to anyone's quest to, "accomplish the extraordinary." Let me explain three important points using firefighting context.

1. You Have To See What You Can't See, Better Than If You Actually Saw It!

Television network programming provides an inaccurate visualization of firefighting and realistic fire conditions. I find it amusing to watch various firefighters perform interior fire attacks on massive blazes as they jump through pockets of fire as ceilings and floors collapse to save potential victims that they spot from across the room or down the hall. Certain fire facts are ignored and clear lines are blurred for the public's viewing pleasure. The fundamental truth that should be known is that most of what you see is not realistic and oftentimes not possible. Firefighters learn to operate in conditions of complete darkness. Smoke eliminates visibility and firefighters are left to rely on countless numbers of training hours to navigate successfully through blacked-out environments that fires create while maintaining a sense of position and direction. Firefighters learn to search for the seat of fires, conduct search and rescue operations, use tools, operate equipment and manipulate their personal protection equipment without the luxury of sight. They execute with high-functioning effectiveness and efficiency. They approach each situation with a tenacious determination to achieve their desired objective, not because they can see it, but because they are forced to visualize success. The reward lies not in their visual ability to see the goal during the process, but in the glory of seeing the world the way they envision after the objective is achieved. No other option exists than to make it come to pass, regardless of how dark, smoky, hot or dangerous the obstacles may be that stand in their way. They "sell out" to the concept of success as if their lives depend on it because they understand that it really does.

The majority of my first month in the fire academy was spent training in settings of complete darkness or wearing a mask that had been painted black to eliminate visibility. Firefighters must gain a level of comfort, familiarity and calmness operating in dark and dangerous environments and develop proficiency and consistency of flawless execution in volatile situations. That's a time-consuming process that requires a daily regimen of training and preparation throughout the course of a career. We trained for the worst and prepared to be the best. On any given day, we would risk our lives to save others. At any given time we might be forced to perform a heroic action that others dare not attempt. At a moment's notice, we might be called to, "accomplish the extraordinary!"

The first month of training in the academy was known as the "weeding out" period. It was the initial stage of separating the pretenders from the contenders, those enamored with the idea of being firefighters from those who possessed the ability to make it through the process. Many people bow out after their first exposure to the heat, flames and stress of what life will look like as a firefighter. Few people adjust and adapt well to stressful operating conditions in general. The addition of complete darkness creates another dimension of complexity and frustration that often proves too much to handle. Some people panic and freak out, others never find focus, while fear paralyzes others until they give up altogether. The successful candidates uncover the internal fortitude and develop the mental toughness necessary to make it through this phase. Those who don't won't. Developing the capacity to see and function without visual sight is the determining factor.

I am not suggesting that anyone commence running into burning buildings to prove their metal, but I believe that everyone's burning desire to achieve a significant level of greatness will produce similar environments. The road to "extraordinary" supplies stressful situations and creates complex and chaotic circumstances that represent the fire conditions in your life. The path to greatness fosters frustration as you develop a proficiency and consistency of flawless execution in volatile conditions. You must locate an internal fortitude and develop a mental toughness to pursue a dream, a vision of success and the desired outcome that you can't see and at times question whether it is attainable. You must persevere; exercising a blind faith in your ability to achieve what you know is waiting.

The commonly heard phrase, "seeing is believing," refers to the capacity to see something in its physical manifestation to believe its existence or possibility. That popular saying is not applicable to dreaming. Visual sight provides a level of comfort and security not available to a dreamer. Dreamers see outcomes that non-dreamers cannot, do not or never will. Visualize "what you can't see, better than if you actually saw it." That vision provides the vehicle that will drive you through the hazardous conditions that are standing in between you and accomplishing the extraordinary.

2. Stay Low And Keep Crawling

Firefighters willfully enter each encounter with a limited amount of time at their disposal to accomplish their objectives. The air contained in the breathing tanks carried on their backs offer a brief supply of air to breathe. Rapidly deteriorating fire conditions can further shorten the period of time in which they have to work. Volatility is constant, making each passing moment unpredictable. Firefighters understand the value of time and the pressing urgency to accomplish objectives within tight parameters better than most. When fire conditions change, strategies shift and plans alter, one tactic remains relatively consistent; stay low and keep crawling.

The phrase, "Stay low and keep crawling," summarizes the process of survival. It describes the unyielding commitment and persistence required to survive the toughest conditions, situations and circumstances thrown your way as you strive to accomplish extraordinary feats. The phrase represents a mindset, a never quit, "die-trying" mentality that eliminates complacency and half-hearted approaches to goal accomplishment. It embodies nerves of steel and guts on steroids. It echoes the sentiment of the sixth President of the United States, John Quincy Adams, who stated, "Courage and perseverance have a magical talisman, before which difficulties disappear and obstacles vanish into air." "Stay low and keep crawling" reflects the grit and determination of a winner.

"Stay low and keep crawling" describes the daily firefighting operational grind. But, that phrase is also applicable to your life and your quest to accomplish the extraordinary. You have a limited amount of time at your disposal to fulfill the big dreams that you have dared to dream. What will you accomplish before life slips away? As you seek an extraordinary existence, get ready to experience fire conditions (if you haven't already). Situations will get hot, steamy and sticky, causing you to sweat, strain and suffer. You will doubt yourself and your ability to emerge victorious, losing sight of the perfect dream that has been the source of your motivation. You may be willing to roll over and succumb to the smoke-filled environments that you find suffocating. But don't. I urge you to stay low and keep crawling. Don't get caught up in the toxic environment that is swirling around above you in the atmosphere. Stay low, take a deep breath and gather yourself. Breathe! I promise you that there is air! Keep crawling. Claw your way through to an extraordinary ending.

3. Find A Way!

Life doesn't come with a roadmap or a solutions handbook. You do not and will not know the answers for everything that you'll encounter regardless of how hard you train or prepare. However, you'll be forced to find solutions on a regular basis and figure things out along the way for survival. Be creative. Be resourceful. The definition of resourcefulness is the ability to analyze quickly situations and leverage the best-suited options at your disposal. But resourcefulness also requires the deliberate movement towards an alternate route to success when the original plan is no longer an option.

The phrase, "Find a way," speaks to the mental resolve that you won't allow yourself to be defeated, no matter what! Despite the degree of difficulty, restriction or constraint, you'll find a way to accomplish your goal. The legendary college basketball coach John Wooden said, "Don't let what you cannot do, interfere with what you can do." In other words, don't let personal or situational limitations prevent you from tapping into available means to prosper. Focus on what will allow you to succeed instead of being intimidated or accepting defeat as a plausible option. The challenges may be bigger, stronger and faster than you feel equipped to handle, but you are able! Dig deep within yourself to find a way!

The great motivational speaker Les Brown, stated, "The graveyard is the richest place on earth, because it is here that you will find all the hopes and dreams that were never fulfilled, the books that were never written, the songs that were never sung, the inventions that were never shared, the cures that were never discovered, all because someone was too afraid to take that first step, keep with the problem, or determined to carry out their dream." How will your story end? Will you contribute to the richness of the graveyard or exhaust every internal reserve so that the treasures you leave established on earth and in others accurately reflect the accurate measure of your wealth? Evaluate your standing. If you haven't fulfilled your destiny and accomplished the extraordinary, find a way!

REFERENCES

Allen, J. (1924). As a Man Thinketh. Girard, Kan: Haldeman-Julius Co.

Anderson, P (1997). Great Quotes from Great Leaders, United States: The Career Press, Inc.

Angelou, M (1993). Wouldn't Take Nothing for My Journey Now. New York: Bantam

Bartlett, J & O'Brien, G (2012). Bartlett's Familiar Quotations. United States: Little, Brown & Company

Brown, L (n.d.) Retrieved from https://www.goodreads.com /quotes/884712-the-graveyard-is-the-richest-place-on-earth-because-it

Consolers, (1969). May The Work I've Done Speak For Me. United States: Nashboro

Clear, J. (2014). Rome Wasn't Built in a Day But They Were Laying Bricks Every Hour, Huffington Post. Retrieved from http://www.huffingtonpost.com/james clear/motivation_b_4935330.html

177

Cynic. (n.d.) *Merriam-Webster.com.* Retrieved July 30, 2014, from http://www.merriam-webster.com/dictionary/cynic

D. C. Comics (Writer) (1977). The All-New Super Friends Hour. Hanna Barbera (Executive producer), United States, *Warner Brothers Television.*

Disney, W. (2015), retrieved from http://www.disneydreamer.com/walt/quotes.htm

Einstein, A. (n.d.). Retrieved from http://www.quotes.net/authors/Albert%20Einstein

Hahn, D. (Producer), Allers, R. & Minkoff, R. (Directors). (1994). The Lion King. United States: Disney.

Henley, W. E. (1893). A book of verses. New York: Scribner.

Hughes, L., Rampersad, A., & Roessel, D. E. (1994). The collected poems of Langston Hughes. New York: Knopf.

Imagination. (n.d.). *Merriam-Webster.com* Retrieved August 10, 2014, from http://www.merriam-webster.com/dictionary/ imagination

Keller, J. (2002). The Mysterious Ambrose Redmoon's Healing Words. Chicago Tribune, Retrieved from http://articles.chicagotribune.com/2002-0329/features/0203290018_1_chicago-police-officer-terry-hillard-courage

Lister, T (2015). Burial Site of 'Don Quixote' Author Miguel de Cervantes Confirmed. CNN, Retrieved from:http://www.cnn.com/2015/03/17/living/feat-cervantes-bones-found/

Martinez, L (2011, June). Access to Independence, *Giving Back Magazine, 38*

Maxwell, J. C. (2007). The 21 Irrefutable Laws of leadership: Follow them and people will follow you. Nashville, Tenn: Thomas Nelson.

Optimism. (n.d.) *Merriam-Webster.com* Retrieved July 30, 2014, from http://www.merriam-webster.com/dictionary/ optimism

Peale, N.V. (2003). The Power of Positive Thinking. New York: Simon & Schuster

Pericles (n.d.). Retrieved from https://www.goodreads.com/quotes/397136-what-you-leave-behind-is-not-what-is-engraved-in

Possibility. (n.d.). *Merriam-Webster.com* Retrieved

July 30, 2013, from http://www.merriam-
webster.com/dictionary/ possibility

Roosevelt, T (n.d.). Retrieved from
http://www.theodorerooseveltcenter.org/Learn
-
About-TR/TR-Quotes.aspx

Rossetti, D (n.d.). Retrieved from
https://www.goodreads.com/author/quotes/101
643.Dante_Gabriel_Rossetti

Rotman, L (2015). 1000 Inspirational Quotes That
Make You Think.

Tzu, L (n.d.), Retrieved from
https://www.goodreads.com/quotes/7459328-
watch-your-thoughts-they-become-words-
watch-your-words-they

U.S. Declaration of Independence, Paragraph 2
(1776).

Kerpen, D. (2014, February). 15 Quotes to Inspire
Great Teamwork, Inc. Magazine. Retrieved
from http://www.inc.com/dave-kerpen/15-
quotes-to-inspire-great-team-work.html

Also available by Jimmy McMikle:

HEY BIG BOY
A MESSAGE TO A SON

"Hey Big Boy" is a must read book to boys of all ages. It is a conversation that speaks to the hearts and minds of our next generation of male greatness. Beautifully illustrated with pictures in watercolor paint, the author has captured a message that provides timeless words of wisdom that every boy needs to hear his parents, caretakers, or loved ones say.

AVAILABLE ON AMAZON.COM

Also available by Jimmy McMikle:

HEY BIG GIRL
A MESSAGE TO A DAUGHTER

"*Hey Big Girl,*" is a powerful message to girls of all ages. Its life directional content offers a solid foundation to develop strong, confident, courageous, and wise young ladies. This book is illustrated in a watercolor paint medium that reflects the beauty of the message itself.

AVAILABLE ON AMAZON.COM

ABOUT THE AUTHOR

P owered by the passionate belief that everyone can achieve greatness, and driven by the opportunity to spark significant, powerful change, Jimmy regularly inspires audiences of children, college students, educators, parent groups, and professionals alike bridging the gap between current positioning and desired direction.

Jimmy is a respected leadership consultant, accomplished author and sought after motivational speaker and life coach. Three simple, yet powerful words define his mission, and direct his passion to equip people for success: **Educate, Inspire, & Empower!** He is President of The McMikle Group, a leadership training and development company. Jimmy's two children's books, "Hey Big Boy" and "Hey Big Girl," provide powerful life directional messages to youth of all ages. He is the founder of the D.R.E.A.M. NOW Program, an intensive youth leadership program whose mission is "to develop responsible, educated, adaptive minds for future leadership."

www.iamjimmymcmikle.com
www.themcmiklegroup.com
www.johncmaxwellgroup.com/jimmymcmikle

36572992R00104

Made in the USA
Middletown, DE
17 February 2019